POETRY now

In My Mind

Edited by

Heather Killingray

First published in Great Britain in 2004 by
POETRY NOW
Remus House,
Coltsfoot Drive,
Peterborough, PE2 9JX
Telephone (01733) 898101
Fax (01733) 313524

SB ISBN 1 84460 767 4

Foreword

Although we are a nation of poets we are accused of not reading poetry, or buying poetry books. After many years of listening to the incessant gripes of poetry publishers, I can only assume that the books they publish, in general, are books that most people do not want to read.

Poetry should not be obscure, introverted, and as cryptic as a crossword puzzle: it is the poet's duty to reach out and embrace the world.

The world owes the poet nothing and we should not be expected to dig and delve into a rambling discourse searching for some inner meaning.

The reason we write poetry (and almost all of us do) is because we want to communicate: an ideal; an idea; or a specific feeling. Poetry is as essential in communication, as a letter; a radio; a telephone, and the main criterion for selecting the poems in this anthology is very simple: they communicate.

Contents

BURY MY HEART

I need a grave to bury my bleeding heart,
Blood seeps through the ground
And stains the soil.
I'll find a friend to carry my load,
A lover to crack my heart of stone,
Like a thief in the night,
To steal my soul.
Someone to break me
And give pain a fresh hold,
I need someone to carry me home.

Festering relationships,
Pulse with anger,
The Devil dances to our song.
Words a knife that cannot be blunted,
Passion a weapon of mass destruction.
Flames leap on her naked hatred
And pain spews from my bitter soul.
Love is a hunger.
I just need someone to help carry my load.

I need a coffin,
To lay this relationship to rest,
Capricious destiny has headed west.
Fill in the grave, start on a fresh one,
Ready for the flesh,
She'll strip my bones.
My heart beats fainter
I feel no more pain
I just needed someone carry my love home.

Kevin O'Gorman

TOURISTS

Why did they build the Castle
so near to *London's* Heathrow?
Surely they must have realised
it's in the air that aircraft go!
Why was it built upon a hill
in blocks of dark grey stone?
The steepness really makes me ill
our roads are straight at home
and such narrow slits for windows
and none of them have glass.
The fashion isn't modern
how were such plans ever passed?

Windsor has its tourists
that have a lot to say
and such knowledge from the purists
astound many every day.
It's a pity William the Conqueror
before his time to go,
overlooked that *London's* aircraft
would have to fly from Heathrow!

D R Thomas

What If

What if the sun
never shone?
What if the grass
never grew?
What if the birds
never sang?
What if the
steeple lay idle
and the church
bells never rang?
What if I had
never met a girl
like you?
What if my
dreams never
came true?
Then all would
be obscurity.

David A Bray

May Love And Blossoms

May blossoms sprinkle under your feet
And move your mood to a lighter beat
May love shine from moonbeams overhead
And guardians guide that love to bed
Itself into the groove of unconscious
          Ever free, ever youth, ever be.

Sharon Grimer

Fool's Paradise

Lining the publican's pockets
And the ever-bulging bookie's till
Flashing lights of fruit machines
Searching for that thrill
That spill that feeds addiction
On the up, raising one more
Amber cup to Bacchus
Hedonism and the like
'Today's the day for a lucky strike' -
Fool's paradise, clouded head
Come tomorrow, no change by the bed
To even buy that loaf of bread.

Sylvia Ross

I'LL BE BOBBY MOORE

The shout rang out, shrill and clear,
'I'll be Bobby Moore!' I shrieked with pride and glee

This was my youth, with gates as goals and a casey ball as a best friend
Hours we would play, next goal's in and round the post -
headers 'n' volleys.
Until the darkness fell and through the gloom Bobby Moore scored
Gordon Banks left stranded, on the pavement all forlorn and gate left
swinging by a screamer of a goal
Geoff Hurst went to ask for the ball back from the next door
neighbour's yard
Before he had to go in for his tea when the ref's whistle sounded
the end of 'play'
In the form of my dad - his fingers in his mouth and a piercing shriek
Which echoed down the avenue inviting me home -
Oh how *that* whistle carried so much earnest meaning,
For in for tea I had to be, Bobby Moore or no Bobby Moore . . .
And alas in for tea I ran - realising that I was me.

And in for tea went Geoff and Gordon and sometimes Greavsie too . . .
Just until tomorrow when Bobby Moore would return and rattle the
gates again with the sound of leather on metal . . .

Today I see no kids - not out and playing?
Loitering, bored - gangs of youths, windows breaking,
Vandalism, graffiti and joyriding abound

Alcohol and drugs replacing gates and leather caseys
Looks of frustration and rage across their faces . . .

If only I could show them what my childhood memories are . . .
But I fear they're gone for good, those days of innocent play
And when he died I fear that more than Bobby died that day . . .

‘I’ll be Bobby Moore . . .’ *David Beckham* maybe now
But leather on metal gates is rarely heard today
And for a one time Bobby Moore . . . alas, just in my memory it
will stay . . .

David Mark Evans

Fathers, Mothers, Sisters, Brothers

Lord send your angels oh so fast, they are needed in a mercy dash,
Tortured souls are in despair, pushed from their bodies, no time
to spare,
Fear hits hard, screams fill the air, pain and sorrow everywhere,
If I could just hold out my hand and try so hard to understand,
Oh Mother, how I feel your pain, your child to never see again,
And Father, how can you count your loss? Your child has gone
at such a cost,
Heartbreak, tears, death and dying, how can these people ease
their crying?
No one can remain untouched, such sadness is widespread,
September 11 2001 etched inside everyone's head,
Each person that has had a loss on that heartbreaking day,
Need somewhere that they can go to sit in thought and pray,
To sit close where their loved ones died and think that they are by
their side, great comfort this would bring,
This place just cannot be rebuilt, the ground where loved ones' blood
was spilled,
Where will all the people go for those who have no graves to show,
America is brave and will go on, God bless those who perished,
September 11 2001.

Ellen Chambers

If Only You Could See

(Dedicated to Faye Marsden)

I wore this around my neck - Faye
I remember I read it to you one day
I kept telling you and showing you
It was even hung on my bedroom wall:

Grant me the serenity
to accept the things
I cannot change.
Courage to change the things I can
and the wisdom to know the difference.
Courage to change the things I can
I thought you'd finally understand
whenever I held your hand
these little pearls of wisdom
how I prayed they'd make a difference
but still you couldn't change
the pattern you just rearranged.

I still pray one day you will see
the serenity prayer wasn't just for me
when we read it in each other's company.

Graham Hare

Talking To Myself Again

Saturdays now sadder days.
Says who? Says I.
Yesterdays, many days, any days will do,
Than these thoughtful, fraughtful Saturdays alone.
Here without you.

Talk away! Not walk away.
Says who? Says I.
That way is hope, don't be a dope.
Don't slide down that 'indifference' slope.
It isn't easy, not at all.
Be mindful of that easy fall.

You will not cope!
I cannot cope?
Says who?
Says I!

Bryan Hackett

Ma Fille

An adult afraid to give
A soul iced over
So much damage done
A difficult lover.
Suddenly there she was
a light to his dark
smiling arms open
leaving her sweet mark.
Love given so unconditional
Rocked foundations thought immutable.
Watching in awe
at her guile
impossible to object
not to smile.
I know his love for me struggled
Distrust he rose above
But in my heart exists no doubt
She always was his first love.

Carol Esslemont

Doing Wrong

What if I've done wrong
The things I said untrue
That I have made a liar
Out of you.
What if I've done wrong
For you've lied in the past
The only thing I ask
Is the truth at last.
What if I've done wrong
In blaming you for more,
Do you think it helps
When you walk out the door.
What if I've done wrong
In accusing you
All you have to answer
That it's all untrue.
But even then suspicions
Of lies that are said,
What if I was wrong
On the day we wed.

J Lanigan

DISILLUSIONED

You were the one that inspired love, that wondrous, ethereal dream
Causing me to care and comfort you (oh, now I could scream!)
Nothing else mattered as long as I was your partner
That longing increased, you were eventually my desire
Love sought me out all alone to become my master
Into that abyss I let myself be cast, you - yes you alone was the guide
Following you there was no fear or dread, reaching perfection
You discovered the isle where we tarried reassuringly
Supplying lots of attention, perfection was totally inbred

Those iced cold lips sealed our union like marbleised stone
Though I longed for this elopement but now wished I'd stayed at home
Love told me I was fickle and implied I had a cruel temperament
I banished further advances and woke restored, no further
Encumbrances

Yes you did infuse my longing especially in dreams
I sought to take advantage as concerned all seemed
Dismissing all foolish gossip as I was whisked away
With you beside me, showing love to guide and always stay
I looked upon you as my all, now suddenly realise
You attempted to make me an example, I had no wish to
become petrified
So cold you were towards me as I strongly disapprove of being
Transformed into ice and viewed in the nude
I changed my mind, it's my prerogative, oh I am so glad to say
You are disappointed and you will not visit and not stay
I always thought that love the charmer, was perfection and sweet
Not ever wishing to become an iced maiden, thank goodness
I wake from haunted sleep

R D Hiscoke

Together Twenty Years

Love has many fickle ways,
how we danced for hours
and fought for days.
The highs and lows,
the days we prayed.
When you laughed as I left
and cried when I stayed.
We've seen it all,
time and time again,
We rode out the happy
as we begged for the pain.
We've both tried to end it
but still we endure,
Going hell for leather
not knowing what the hell for!

M Morris

Skin Deep

Horror and crime and out of time,
Ranking first was man, not A-bomb slime.
Blood spilled like water,
Or re-phrasing that, exactly water.
Bombs packed with nails,
Remember the guts and entrails!
A limb that doesn't match,
Like a stork with no foot.
Safety always first,
The chronic outburst.
Steel-jacketed bullets scrawl
That's paid you not to brawl.
Hypochondriacs, psychopaths,
Choose like we, for life or doom.
Justice pays for peace
To repeat is to say no to deceit
Or be pulled down the dirty, old street.

Hardeep Leader

DECORATING

It's time to decorate the house,
Time to make a start.
The 'wood effect' wall must come down.
With the fireplace I must part.

'Start with a blank canvas.'
The experts always say.
But I can't replace my 'cherry' wall,
So the wood effect must stay.

To change the fire surround would be
Disastrous in itself:
Where would all my pot cats go
Without a mantelshelf?

My carpet and my suite are green,
The doors are always white,
The ceiling and the coving too,
Are white to keep them light.

That leaves three walls to decorate.
It must be something mellow.
I fancy something 'lemony',
But they're already yellow!

To change the curtains is the thing,
Perhaps that's what I'll do,
But no, I really can't do that
They're brown and they're brand new.

It's time to decorate the house.
Now isn't that a joke?
Like a US President once said,
'Don't fix what isn't broke!'

Margaret Doherty

CHERIE'S REVENGE

Rob snores quite loudly through the night
Sounds like a cat having a fight!
After a slap on his chin
Or a swift kick to his shin
His snores still carry on through the night

The plaster technique is a sight
Our chemist said, it works quite all right.
With a puff from his lip
He's back on his trip
And his snores still carry on through the night.

I've tried a pillow to muffle my plight
Held down firmly and it was tight!
I've squeezed tight his nose
I've held his mouth tightly closed
Alas, his snores still carry on through the night.

So I lay there awake through the night
In the hopes he stops snoring, well he might.
I lay by his side in a doze
With my hand over his nose
Muffling his snores that go on through the night.

Then at last the snores stop at first light
The sheer peace is much to my delight.
He turns his head facing me
And says, 'Wharro Mon Cherie'
Quite oblivious to his snores through the night.

To all you ladies who suffer the same plight?
Because your hubby snores through the night.
I've got a few painless ideas
With no worries or no fears
So we can all sleep undisturbed through the night.

Pat Thoume

Be True Unto Yourself

I guess the colour of my life
Is not just the sight I hold
It is about the morality I hear
About the friends I meet . . .
I walk my road in life
Through hurts that try to divide
The way that my life thinks
The way it always tries to do best.
I guess the colour of my life
Is there to cheer me - and others . . .
Some take hold and demean
Some smile and realise . . .
The glory in life is there for all of us
Even in the war-torn countries abroad
Each of us has meaning . . . a purpose in our lives
We can either shout at others
Try to change others, hurt others with our own problems
Or, we can accept the life within us
And focus, focus on true worth

Josie Lawson

WEARY

Weary of the road I travel
This journey I wish would end
Wanting through the long night
An answer I could defend

Wary of each stranger
Afraid they will condemn
Silence is all I offer
And this action may well offend

Each footfall takes me further
Each corner round each bend
Along the streets of darkness
My breaking heart descends

Strong words against the moonlight
Flowing freely, not contained
Such remarks can't be altered
This night I lost a friend

Albert Whiteside

The Bone Yard

I was brought here often as a child.
What, I wonder, was the fascination?
Death has visited and left.
Even scavengers find no sustenance.
Yet the remains have been picked over,
Some handled with tender regard,
Some kicked aside in anger.
A spire of old dreams rattles to earth,
Sending up a cloud of despair.
I will not come again.

Janis Simpson

Anniversary Poem

Forty years together
My man and I.
We laugh, love and fight
and care a lot.
Together we can reach the sky
There is no one else -
and yet, in nature's way
Attraction, pulls me
to Those 'hip' young men.
I daydream of some amorous play!
In longing for my lost youth
I see them Prime of Life now topping
But as I tell my real true love -
'I'm only window shopping'.

Ann Way

My World

The cigarette burns close to my sandy hand
And I feel the heat tingle up my arm,
Ignorant of pain and lost in a trail of thoughts,
In my own world.
This is where I love.
Oblivious of reality.
A place of dreams where I don't have to be me
And can be anyone or anything that I want to be.
I push and squeeze this world out making way for my Utopia.
My world.
No one else's.
Mine.
My world is that love you should always feel,
My world is that freedom that should always be felt,
Where the future is clear and no cards can be dealt.
My Utopia bursts and I am back with real life,
Fighting and struggling with strife.
My only lifeline is that time I have alone
Where I can sink into an endless coma of aspirations.
My world.

Nicky Stecker

A MAN!

He started off a tradition that grew so great
Came as a ‘stranger’ to become a ‘mate’
Served time in prison for doing wrong
Entertained the inmates with stirring song
Sang ‘western’ ditties with a touch of ‘blues’
Never afraid to express his views
A western favourite from way down south
A wealth of chart toppers came from his mouth
Those charts were rocked by his bold, hard style
Yet he warmed our hearts with his big broad smile
O’er the plains to sing he would often plod
Made a complete turnabout when he turned to God
His stroll across the ‘boards’ is now at an end
We have lost not only a legend but, too, a friend
A reason to remember him? It is just this
His presence in this world we shall sorely miss
He sold his soul as the rest he’d thrash
‘Goodbye old timer’ - dear Johnny Cash!

Jon El Wright

A Mother's Love

Darling, you know I didn't want you to go
I know it seems that life is so unfair
But please remember that you'll always be my baby
And no matter what, I'll always be there
I will love you more than you will ever know
And darling you will never be on your own
So anytime you want to talk
You've only gotta pick up the telephone

I was always there for you when you were small
And I was the one who would pick you up
To kiss away the tears that you cried
Everytime that you had a fall
And I will be there for you as you get older
Because with each passing day that comes
As you become more beautiful
My love for you will grow more bolder

My darling as your life starts to open up to you
As the guardians of destiny guide you through time
I know your beautiful light will come shining through
And when all and everyone else fails you
The strongest love you will ever feel will be mine
And all the feelings that I have now will emerge in you
One day when you are a mother yourself
You'll realise everything that I have said is true

A mother's love is forever
And nothing can stand in its way
The bonds that we share my darling
Just keep getting stronger
Each and every day

Richard J Byers

Feeling My Dragon

My dragon is always near me,

I feel his love surrounding me with,
  Each cool breath of wind,
  Each warm ray of sunshine,
  Each crystal drop of rain.

I see his love surrounding me with,
  Each colour in the rainbow,
  Each delicate butterfly's wing,
And the tender flower's petal.

I hear his love surrounding me with,
  The sweet note of a bird's song,
  The special sound of a baby's laugh,
And the haunting sound of a wolf's cry.

I sense his love surrounding me with,
  The feeling I'm always being watched,
  The confidence that I should not be afraid,
And with the warmth of his arms wrapped around me.

I am always cherished and protected.

Dan Del'ouest

A Walk Through A Storm

I woke up in the morning, wiped my eyes
And opened my bedroom door to a new world.
I found myself gazing at an icy paradise.
It reminded me of the North Pole.
So I put on my jacket, took two steps out of my door
And all of a sudden, the door slammed shut.
I quickly opened it and then there was nothing there.
I was stranded.
I didn't know what to do.
My heart rate started rising. I was terrified.
I then walked for about an hour. I was starving.
Luckily I found an igloo full of food.
I went inside and had a big feast.
After that I nodded off to sleep.
When I woke up I found myself back in my bedroom.

Danny Morgan

THE FUTURE IS BRIGHT

We are living in the 21st century.
The Space Age.
Where
Murder
Rape
Poverty
Famine
Torture
And war
Wear silver Spandex jump-suits and have flashing lights.
It's just how we imagined it.

Doug Cairns

INLAND AIRSHOWS POEM

As now we see an aeroplane fly at Duxford, taking
off from the runway, flying up high into the sky,
and up there look, a machine which looks like a bird.
It's not a bird, it's a plane, and noise determines
that and that aeroplane flies higher, higher in the sky,
higher in the sky, viewing the aeroplanes as they fly.
So we walk around, more aeroplanes taking off and flying around,
people standing staring still, many of them walk around,
some the length of the runway. Now we see another
aeroplane fly, taking to the sky, in long lengths of
fly, passes on by, airshows again North Weald and
Biggin Hill, airshows, airshows, aeroplanes fly over
manoeuvre of actions to displays, aeroplane flies
right up high into the clouds, looking smaller
then gets to fly around, nearer to the people
standing on the ground and look its size better.
So as we walk around, more aeroplanes parked on
the ground and an aeroplane that's higher, higher in
the sky, higher in the sky. As we are viewing the
aeroplanes now that fly on by, people standing staring
still, many then walk around. Aeroplanes in the
sky, until the show comes to an end.
Aeroplanes landing, aeroplanes flying off, and people
with cars parked have left and on the road
going home.

Robert A Gould

This Summer

I've loved the days
This summer
Have done so much it seems
Sunny days
The parks, the beach
It's really been a dream
Sad that too soon
It will end
Just winter days
Just round the bend
I hate to think
Of cold wet days
Or winds that blow
Your hat away
Longing to stay
By the fire
The evenings all
Too long by far
I guess my thoughts
Just on a whim
Will think how lovely
Summer's been

Jeanette Gaffney

IN A PSYCHIATRIC UNIT

The locked ward - House B
It was more like a prison
With its paved courtyard
Where one would pace up and down
Whilst the 'jailers' upon us frowned
Little wonder Van Gogh cut off his ear
Methinks to get away from people who
mockingly came too near;
Four stood close around me
Each with the same taunting cry
'Go to your room - take your medication'
I wanted to curl up and die:
Tim, one of the 'jailers' wrenched me by my
left shoulder
Then hurled me against my bedroom wall - *whack!*
Felt like a skinned cat!
So merciless was he - such utter cruelty.
Scared out of my wits
Could not rest - could not sleep
How thankful was I when after a week
To be moved from that fateful House B
to House D.

Gwyneth E Scott

THROUGH THE HARD YEARS

Life's been hard for me over the years
As now I hear that sound through my ears.
Spent past nine years just being sick
Now I hobble with my walking stick.
Look out my window at cloudy skies
Through now a pair of almost dimming eyes.
From breakfast right up to my tea
I spend my time writing my poetry.

Still I'm lucky for one my age
I have put more poetry onto a page.
A thousand poems now I have in print
Still not bad seeing I'm old and skint.
There are plenty worse off than me
So I hope my poems lots of folk see.
For one who is semi-disabled
I hope my poems one day will be fabled.

Thank God for them at Arrival Press
I'm just another lucky poet I guess.
From the night darkness to the bright day
In my poetry I have plenty to say.
Like many with my aches and moans
The thought male members don't make old bones.
Still, even if one day I then am gone
Through Arrival Press my poetry will live on.

Colin Allsop

WORSE THAN OPENING NIGHT

Ultra violet vanishing point
within darkest, ragged surround
pulsating, burning cascade of
quicksilver rain falling like
glass beads; back off, keep still.

The silent auditorium a creation
of abated breath and jangling nerves.
The show is about to start, you wait,
there's no help now, you're on your own.
Don't touch this too tangible precipitation.

Backstage the wit is caustic,
eyes burning from over exposure to 'feel'.
Recalcitrance no protection against
forced urbane repartee, vituperation
fired off by vitriolic rheum, ricket

inducing reviews. Those who can't write . . .
they'll have you in stitches . . .
mostly dropped. Chain stitches, chain
mail, fettering. Chain letter with about
as much charm. Pass it on or die.

Raw emotion, raw energy, raw invective.
Where the chrysanthemum, Vesuvius,
the Catherine wheel? Where the thrust
and parry? Oh, they're sparking off
all right. If only they were on the stage.

Philip Beverley

We Are The Darkness

You look at us
as if there is something wrong with us,
You don't realise
the difference
between good and evil,
You can't distinguish
between black and white,
darkness equals evil
or so you believe.

We are the darkness
yet we don't follow the Devil
and yet you call us evil,
We dress in black
and don't follow your ways
so you call us evil.

You fear what you don't understand
and you hate what you fear,
so you brand us evil
and you lynch us up,
You don't understand our ways
so you call us evil,
we are the darkness.

Corwin Barber

THE SOUL

But what of the soul,
That, which we grow,
All that we know,
Its seeds that we sow.

But what of the mind,
That, which we use,
All that we choose,
Not to be abused.

But what of the body,
That, which we neglect,
All that we protect,
And that we have wrecked.

But what of the Earth,
The place of our birth.

Paul Leslie

Fit For Something

Number's up, have we got your attention?
Cheating the Devil against high odds
Peaks and troughs - well done; shame,
Blame, guilt, failure, not all your own.

You are well now, it's psychosomatic
All in the mind, singing that song
A key you did find
Alcohol is your danger zone

In a mixed salad of past
Beware that devil-may-care,
It is not the case -
That devil pushes in all haste.

Slow it down, read the lie of the land
Do not scorn a helping hand;
Listen to others whinge
Whilst out on a binge.

Morning breaks hung over in self abuse
Fit for something -
Fit for nothing, after all
It was your call.

Christopher Dixon

THE CHAIRS

Two chairs not empty
Two friends never left
A path of thoughts
Blue skies and songbirds

Tears and laughter shared
peace and calm there
light shines within the soul
Friendship given in harmony

Two chairs not empty
two friends never left
Blue skies with birds in song
A path of thoughts.

As you walk and talk
Remembering the joy
As time you passed
Never lost never sad

So when you look
the chairs you see
Are the friends
We will always be.

R Mills

Breaking Strain

(For Julia)

Soft whispers fall on silent ground
Whilst all around
Echoes from the past are found
Carelessly bound.

Nothing is done, nothing is said
A haunting dread
Playing games inside your head
Anger flows red.

Words said in undertones of lies
Meaningless cries
A strong friendship slowly dies
Saying goodbyes.

No tomorrow will make amends
Time just ends
Sharply like some modern trends
As truth offends.

A bitter lesson, you are blameless
Direction so aimless
Old pictures now appear frameless
People stay nameless.

Young dreamers have grown apart
A broken heart
One will remain, one will depart
Make a new start.

Life still holds so much my dear
Sense no fear
You will succeed, see things clear
Shed no tear.

George S Johnstone

I Believe

Sometimes life holds more valleys than hilltops
More promise than burning pain
Let fears of life wash over you
When troubled, lost and adrift
Upon a stormy sea and rain

Ups and downs are all an important part of
This entangled web of life we lead
Each one of our fore-planned destinies

There is always a true and loyal
Friend to help you through
The challenges of life

He walks beside you day by day
Helps you in all your troubles
Guides you on your way

Mary Veronica Ciarella Murray

WAKING NEWS

Mild May's morning light
diffuses through the sleep
and focuses the prospects
as larkspur nods in the garden.

The radio penetrates
as the diurnal rhythm develops.
Local burglary, fire, assault are news
but the world of family and money
determines our actions.

Deaths elsewhere make news.
Ten assassinated in Karachi.
Sixteen bombed in Jerusalem.
Deaths by number, not people.
Less important?
Less relevant to our humanity
though families cry in the streets?

The sun sparkles on high cypress
and our selfish little lives proceed.

Fleming Carswell

FOR WHAT?

Baghdad.
A concrete tomb,
For mother and for child,
For unknown soldiers of all sides,
For what?

Brian Fahy

ROMNEY

I want to get back
To the Downs and the spires
From the Romney vales
And the sea front of years
From the mists of the pastures
The fields full of sheep
The chickens and goat herds
And seagulls flying steep
From the trains on the railway
The cars near the piers
I want to get back
To the Downs and the spires.

Peter Buss

No More Hot Dinners

No more hot dinners
For workers at 4 West
Only sandwiches and rolls
Or microwaved meals at best

No more paying £10 up front
Every Monday morning
Spend as little as we choose
For food to stop us yawning

Some order lunch from a shop
But they must ask their foreperson
To get it for them in exchange
For payment to this person

Only those going to college
Will have a plated knife and fork meal for selves
Paid for at the counter
Which they have not brought there themselves.

H G Griffiths

The Ice Maiden

Internet lines brushing those curly-whirly dreams:
Ying-yang antithesis in Bohemian culture,
A myriad of . . . things: 'all is not what it seems';
'Can't get me head round it'; 'l'enfer, c'est les autres'.

Gentle tanning globe, glimpse of a maybe;
If only, if only, so lonely indeed.
Stiff soul blue, daydreams that sting, frost-bitten sores.
A thought of such purity,
An act of depravity.
Lost ember shadows a vamp bewitching,
Goose down sparkling, ecstasy in flight,
Covering all in frozen sameness,
White, a hint of white.

Their vaporised snorts crawl excitedly over her ice-wizened memories,
Drip, drip, dripping.
Frantic lights flicker spellbound northern
Against industrial alienation:
A harsh harshness engaging, contrasting rich tones and
Her long path to treachery.
Was she here?
Was she here, when they passed unsighted in purpose?
Was she here, for all she has lived?
Is she here? And how much remains for her still to learn?

'On rate toujours sa vie': les jeux sont faits.
Thanks Jean-Paul, but until that day . . .
. . . if only, if only, so lonely
The Ice Maiden whose heavy perfumed swallows moist, frenzied seed:
Our thoughts, reasons, knowledge and dreams.

Ian Lowery

ANGEL MESSAGES

Oh the limits and frustrations of life
Only those with MS really know.
Frustration, frustration and more frustration,
Angels give me patience!

When things are just out of reach
When things are just too heavy
And when one's strength gives out
Angels give me patience!

Stop me swearing, give me strength
Let me laugh and make me smile
Life could be much, much worse
Angels give me patience!

I could be dying of cancer
As many friends have done
Instead I am merely housebound
Angels give me patience!

But I have a fabulous view
Always there, changing during the day
Also I have seven grandchildren
So what am I grumbling about?

Angels have given me patience
So I will survive and enjoy myself
Life could be far, far worse
I have much to thank the angels for.

Eve Eckstein

SEPTEMBER SONG

I love it when the autumn creeps
Across the distant hill,
Oh so shyly first she peeps
And breathes her evening chill.
The nights draw in a little more
As summer slowly dies,
What will winter have in store
Before the spring does rise.

As sweet September sings her song
Grey morning mists are seen,
The watery sun no longer strong
A landscape no longer green.
For suddenly on that distant hill
The autumn's colours glow,
Leaves of gold and russet thrill
And scarlet berries grow.

So listen to September's song
When she sings for you,
With winter close it won't be long
Till frozen morning dew.
I love it when the autumn peeps
Across the misty hill,
This is the time that summer sleeps
Awaiting winter's chill.

Marisa Greenaway

TRANSITION?

Here comes adulthood
Watch out before you
Lose yourself completely
Let it be understood
You did everything you could
To keep your child spirit free.

Wish I had a map that
Could get me on my way
Back to never-never land
But it doesn't look like I can
No matter what I say
No one will understand.

I won't be backed into
A corner and forced
To be something I'm not
Me and my childhood,
Not ready for divorce.

June Craven

OUROBOROS

I float over dusty flats
unaware of its approach - suffusing
an infinitesimal tongue across
a meal of a million miles.

It comes. Moving effortlessly between the gaps,
sweeping between the void - cycloning beneath.
Stroking space.
It is infinite.
Hear it laugh as I curve away.
I am nothing.
Swallow.

Carry along its saddle spine,
whispering the cold.

Moving effortlessly between the gaps.
Sweeping down galaxies - bridging time.
Follow.

Invites you in, eyes growing narrow slits.
Consumes futile endeavours.
Contests time, licks past the breathless light.

Let it chase me for I am endlessly circling.
Strangled down a restricted tract.
Contemptuously I am dropped
. . . an icy aurora.

Briony Dennis

TIME BIRD

For you time bird,
I sang sad words.
You broke my weary wings,
So I banged bad words.
It can't be undone,
All the twists and turns,
All my loving flames,
Leaving scars from the painful burns.

What can I do?
Where do we go?
Am I lost forever,
Where the cold winds blow?
You aren't there,
Anymore.
All seems cold and bare,
I see the snow at my door.

I thought I knew,
Where I was going.
A river of love to you,
Trickling and gently flowing.
I thought we were perfect,
But you time bird have flown,
And now I know,
I have never known.

I have never known,
Though I believed you were true.
Yes, I have never known,
Who are you?
I never knew you,
Though I thought I did.
You never showed me,
You always hid.

I thought I did,
But I never heard.
I never knew,
My flown time bird.
I have never known,
Though I believed you were true.
Yes, I have never known,
Who are you?

Carol Ann Darling

ANGELA'S FACE

You take me to celestial realms,
By beauty I am overwhelmed,
This is a trite, prosaic place,
But when I see your lovely face,

Your eyes shine beauty from your soul,
You scorch and sear like white-hot coal,
You're very kind - you are exquisite,
Did I go to Heaven for a visit?

You walk with majesty and grace,
Yes, you enchant me in this place,
I'm helpless - caught within your spell,
Is this where other angels dwell?

So closely guarding Heaven's treasure,
My tenderness I cannot measure,
I am serene and calm like ice,
I catch a glimpse of paradise.

At dusk the skies are tinged with pink,
Of everyone I love, I think,
As night comes in to quench the day,
I pray this feeling's here to stay.

For I can't help it, I adore,
The sweetest girl I ever saw,
You smile so gently, without guile,
So I'm in Heaven for a while.

My faith in humans you renew,
Just breathing air up close to you,
Angelic vision I'm resigned,
To saying your dear soul's divine.

Phil McLynn

LADY LUCK

I've never met her!
Never had the pleasure of
Shaking her privileged golden hand.
Pots of yellow, still lie interned,
Deep at some rainbow's end . . .
Never harvest reaped
The benefit of windfalls.
Starved of diamond-studded halls.

She teases with unfounded promises.
Never delivers that big bonanza,
That lucky antique find.
The lottery of life, draws zero blanks.
Never experienced the full coffers
Of the bullion, bulging banks.

She hides, evades herself of me.
Crosses the paved streets of gold,
When finally we nearly meet.
I am convinced she is ugly,
Hard hearted, unfair in her dispensation
For she has my name written upon her slate.
In the column, opposite the fortunate.

Ian Bowen

ALIENS

Explosions made me and all to be,
As well as the indefinitely space you see is infinitely,
Vast as you or me as human race and life lives that same ecstasy,
But energy does not leave you see as it goes into the infinitely which makes explosions all over and creates IT as intelligence is also infinitely made of me,
Atoms you see which provide the answer to energy's mystery.

James McBeath

NIGHTMARE

I am lying fearless
White cotton sheet under my soul

You face - it is wet
I smell your smell
You call that name
Again and again

We are often here

You in your nightmare
Me - I lay here still
Watching you

A time ago I would wake you
No . . . not now
I let you go to her

Less I learn a little more

Moira Clelland

Relativity

When Albert begun,
He had such fun,
Taking on the cemetery
Assault course run.

So in sacred memory
To those six foot deep,
Above Matthew's grave
He would powerfully leap.

And in loving memory
To those cold in a vault,
Over Mark's resting place
A triple somersault.

In fond remembrance
To those asleep in stone,
Over Luke's weathered tomb
His body was thrown.

And to the everlasting peace
Of those rotting within,
Atop John's headstone
A fine headspring.

And finally a sprint
As fast as he could,
Toward the horizon
Where the Gravedigger stood.

Steve Darlow

Abigail

Abigail, the freak waves soar,
A wind, a dream, a sail.
From your Buddha's heart
A desperate plea
To English shores
Via antique sea
Only drowning in your spell.

Your hennaed hair,
Moroccan flair,
Your simple *joie de vivre.*
The moon may wax and wane,
But constant is the pain,
Of separation
From my beloved still.

Our union of love will be
guided not abated,
By the constellations
we've created.
As for mystics,
Our own yardsticks,
Will thresh the wheat from
the chaff.

Civilisations come and
cultures go,
Abi, draw a line in God's sand.
A simple ceremony,
The breeze in harmony,
We've struggled, humble,
hand in hand.

John Hobbs

MEMORIES

Today I remembered
the wonderful world I have found in your hands . . .
an entirely new and incredible world,
where every caress on my skin
felt like the wind of spring
breathing softly all over it,
and where even the smallest word
was so filled with life that it hurt . . .
I remembered everything,
starting with stars and ending with lightnings
and even more,
roads of passion and roads of pain,
and eyes,
curious eyes,
hungry eyes and also hungry lips . . .
. . . it was all there . . .
. . . and the only proof I have that it was true
is this sweet and painful sensation
of missing you and the world of your hands . . .

Liliana Cucu

SHOOT THE STARS

The fire inside me, volcano boom
You hit me with your tongue,
So sharp, if you were a fish, a swordfish
You would be seen
Don't hit me, for I will fire back,
Now I've got the knack,
On your bike, chuck the Tic Tacs,
Pitter patter to much natter.
See me I'm fine, just passing the time,
Time to time, when I fire back at you,
I will send you back to Venus,
I've got the power to shoot you with the stars,
Don't think it's fun or I will shoot from the sun,
The sun, the stars, not that on Mars,
Get back to the bar, you're going too far,
Chill a bit or I will chuck you in the pit,
You're not fit to hit me with your 'soul',
Underground you go, live with the moles,
Darkness, no life, you're not fit to be my wife,
I don't give a hoot,
For the stars they are going to shoot your heart,
I've got the art, this is my play,
So away you go, take your tongue in tow,
Below, below, you go,
I win, you sin
Now I sin to win, shoot the stars.

Paul Billett

MEMORIES OF JOHN LARSON

It's easy to remember the past.
I think about TV and cider at the Honeysuckle.
He liked his beer, he said it was the antidote.
He didn't want to be a follower - well who does?

He painted pictures and was always afraid.
Dad called home Heaven,
Heaven is home,
Home by the sea.

I don't want to be a richer man.
I want to be a kinder man.
I want to learn how to love.

Alan Cornelius

WILD FLOWER

Fair wild flowers of multi colour,
Your fragrance as sweet as a child's
Sweet demeanour.

You grow beneath the yellow leaves fall,
Oh carrier of life for insects to crawl.
The river flows so near to your edge,
To bring you life, for its soul's sacred pledge.

The sun filters through to give you your strength,
To dance in the wind, and multiply in length.
You spread your beauty for all to see,
So the woods give our race a place to be.

Thank you nature for showing us your story,
It's perfect in form and should take all the glory.
Without your presence life would be much less,
Without your care life would be in a mess.

Ricky N Lock

Scissors

Sharp and quick
Don't give you any warning
They never miss a trick
And here they are again
Just when I'm standing straight
They cut me down like a thousand knives
So sharp, so quick, so hate

But I will rise with the winter sun
So cold, so bold
Like beginnings have begun

Anna Moore

Appledore Sunset

leaden slipping
sucking heat hot
stealing pale light
a griddled sun
fires slate roofs
liquefies
into tomorrow

Neal Moss

Untitled

No status, no work
Just drop out
Regret
Where on earth
Is the safety net?

All the times
All the neglect
Where on earth
Is the safety net?

P Allen

WEATHER HAIKUS

Strong northerly blast
Bitingly cold, snow laden
Straight from the Urals.

Harsh easterly gale
Screams in rage under the door,
Chilling the marrow.

Soft southerly breeze
Gently kisses the tight buds,
Warms them into life.

Wild westerly wind
Seizes the blossoms and strips
Each swaying branch bare.

Christine Akhurst

ROAD TO CRISIS

Backs stiffened by the plough
Unceasing toil, furrowed brows
Taloned hands that work the earth
Destinies prescribed from birth

Numbers lessen year on year
Skills have gone but never fear
Vanished hedges, plundered ponds
Intensive cropping going wrong

Subsidy payments, pesticides
EC quotas, set aside
Nitrates leaching to the sea
Animal feeds bring BSE

The funeral pyres across the land
Meant animal movements were banned
Whilst politicians ignored the cost
A national heritage was lost

The panacea, GM foods!
Another science as yet unproved
Your future is safe we hear them say
Why does it sound like yesterday?

Government policy without shame
Always someone else to blame
The bond with earth is ebbing fast
Our stewardship may not last

No more reasons to explain
Why the country is in pain
Acceptance of the role we've played
Upon the economic stage

We must return to sanity
And heed tomorrow's children's pleas
The responsibility is ours to take
We cannot afford another mistake

Martin Blakemore Davis

Night Wind

Naked branches toss and bend in the gale,
now glowing amber-gold under a street light.
Darkness adds an eerie substance to the wind.
Lamp posts rock, flag poles clang! Clang!
Leaves splat against the windowpane
and dust tinkles like splinters of glass.
Down the chimney an oboe plays.
Empty plant pots scuttle across the lawn.
A crack in a door somewhere whistles like a bird.
Candle flames dance, sizzle and flicker.
The thunderous raw squeezes between the houses
and rages as it breaks free.
The world is singing like a baritone!

Trish Mooney

Snow

She arrives so silently,
flurried, frozen flakes.
She lies down gently,
so sensuous, and soft.
A virgin in her trousseau,
she is cold confetti.
Shapely, chaste and pure
as the driven snow.

Towns, once harsh, are now transformed.
Countryside, once green, veiled in bridal white.
Eyes on the bride, all are in awe.
She is divine. Magnificent.
Prettiest picture of all.

Cats and dogs rain on her with their paws.
Birds peck her cheeks in their quest to find food.
Commuters tread on her - they will never be bound.
She is scarred, also scared.
Unwed, vows unsaid.

A union could slow the groom's pace of life,
But, a ploughing machine casts Miss Snow to one side.
He rubs salt in her wounds; she lies weak in the gutter.
Is the marriage off, perchance, fair maiden?
Oh no - never! Merely postponed . . .

Theresa Mead

SPACEMAN

Powerless as a womb child
He orbits the earth
In a steel ball,
High, high, faraway from the human eye,
A baby planet monarch of nothing
But a God's eye view.
Rocketing for the stars at lift off,
A new world beckoned,
But the cord of communication tells him
He must return.

Gerry McSorley

A White Dove

Strange to place this here -
A strangeness, undeserved,
With no understanding how
And still very unsure why,
The white dove came to visit.

Journeyed to perch alone, untouched, pure of intent,
We shared only a few moments together
Until, questioning overthrew me -
Entering an unfamiliar world, of wonder and of beauty,
In which a message *must* have been sent.
One of freedom? Friendship? Peace, love? Or harmony maybe?
I gestured to care for her, to feed and to nurture her.
How like love, as she's unreceptive still;
She sat alone, untouched and pure of intent.
The only problem is . . . *I* don't really *know* why.
Or maybe, she came to represent *every* possibility,
A grace in the tumult of my excitement,
To show resolved balance, that kept her on that ledge;
Not to look to the sky, not to take flight,
And certainly not to look down.
But to hold her ground,
While all else stare futuristically,
Expectant of such and encounter.

See, she's just a white dove.
Simply. Never to be seen again.
A white dove. No other message to be gained.
Just a sweet contrast to our busy pigeon life.
She left alone, untouched and pure of intent.

Susa Houston

RECOLLECTION

Standing here takes me back

In a hopeless state
I stood here and threw a flower

A red rose

Total silence
All voices drowned out

Every movement is in slow motion
Time almost stands still . . .

Until the flower hits your coffin

Then the cutting realisation hits home
Like running into a brick wall
I see the truth

A wake up call like no other
Facing facts
You are gone
Your body is now buried

But not your soul.

Sarah Moore

BIRTH DAZE

Life begins for us all with a thrust or two,
One of the quickest and easiest things we do.
An act of reproduction is as simple as ABC
And to be successful doesn't require a university degree.

In contrast, the natural consequences which may follow this simple act
Will affect your life with considerable impact.
The wonderful process of development has begun,
All stemming from a few moments of innocent fun.

To marvel at the progressive steps that ensue
Is a process we all automatically do.
But to understand the complexities that take place
Is a task that eludes the majority of the human race.

Nevertheless, generally most parents take pleasure
In creating and producing their 'little treasure'.
Inevitably the wonder of procreation is buried quite deep
As the daily chores ensure that your main desire is sleep.

A Jessop

BLESSINGS

And in the smile
Of a stranger
I feel refreshed,
My faith restored,
Easy to know how
One can lose their way
In this crazy maze
Called life,
Clinging to familiar things
Afraid of letting go
And being alone,
Disguised blessings welcome
With an open heart,
Be sure and take the time
Needed to see
Who you really are.

S Barnard

JUST AN ORDINARY DAY

I met a wonderful lady
just a few weeks ago,
I knew her not before but,
I came to know her so.

Though I didn't know her name,
her love of poetry was just the same.
The spell would often get her out of bed
in the middle of the night,
so as she could then with her loving hand
begin to write.
Words that had so enlightened my
otherwise tiring day,
in the middle of an aisle in the store of
'Safeway's!'

I hoped that we could somehow in the future
keep in touch,
for she had brightened up my day
so very, very much . . .

C Cross

It Takes Time

In London I was born, survived,
St Albans was unknown to me,
In ignorance I lived
Until a cycling club I joined.
One summer's day with spirits high
Off we set to explore our land.
St Albans, one brawny cyclist said,
St Albans is en route today.

Now there's a name I'm sure I've heard!
Vague thoughts of Romans
And early Christians stirred.
Where are we now?
We've reached the Chilterns.
Where is St Albans?
An hour behind us down the road,
You didn't see it girl?

Twenty years or so went by
We'll take them to St Albans
It's a place to know.
Oh, pity, the Abbey's closed.
Now imagine children, this was a theatre -
No! You can't play football here.
Doubtless they will appreciate it,
In a few more years.

Bernadette Cronin

Written The Morning After The Operation

Last year, my youngest son
Became a man,
But last night in the cubicle,
Awaiting the operation,
My son, who is a man, became
My child again.
And I said to my child,
Who is a man,
'Wish that I could take your pain,'
My child replied with tearful smile,
'Dad, I wouldn't wish this pain on you.'
I knew, my child had become a man.

Dec Isaacs

UNTITLED

Life is a good question
but there is no good answer
life is the answer to everything
but there is no question
only how does it happen?
Can you answer that question?
Can you understand life?
If you have the correct question
with the correct answer
then life shall become meaningless.

S Millington

SOUL

I traced the sky
with a white wing
like soft waves upon the clouds,
an angel eye spied upon my flight
to the spirit world
from a place beside
the cool calmness
of the moon,
a glowing orb of light shining
in the darkness
beckoning my soul
deep into the night,
ghosts welcome me
in their shrouded mists
surrounded by death's mystery,
in the depths of this spirit world
there are no secrets.

Louise Lucas

Sam

He came to work on Monday,
He looked a sorry sight,
With one eye rather blackened
And a leg that gave him gyp!

His humour kept him going,
Whilst telling all his story,
Of football at the weekend
And heading balls for goals!

I'm sure that banging heads together,
Is not within the rules,
But then we only have his word
That football was the cause!

He thought he'd torn a tendon,
Or maybe something else,
He even joked and laughed aloud,
'You never know, it could be broken!'

I bet the smile soon faded,
When doctors broke the news,
'Your leg is broken Mr Kettle,
In plaster it will have to go!'

Some have laughed and some have gasped,
But all do wish him well,
That Sam the football manic
Can soon discard his crutches!

Sue Colson

LETTING LOVE GO?

How can I release you?
For I know men's hearts cannot be ripped from their moorings.
Nor can the ever-changing sea batter memory till it has no face.

My heart, it swells with the grief I see before me.
To separate love from nature.
Yet I know release will be your freedom
And with that, the future more wisdom can embrace.

Stand tall with the hungry ocean around you.
Plead with the sky for light.
Grow with the changing sands of time
Away from my eyes.

But let the whispering winds bring news of you.
So my lone heart can beat in time.
And if, perchance to meet again
Smile at me old friend and hold me for a while.

Tell me not of where nature nor love took you.
Rather where fate will steer you next.
And if my eyes and soul are no longer clouded
May I be following to?

Fiona Cashman

My Grandma

Grandma, although you are gone,
You're still with us,
In our memories
And in our hearts.

We all love you,
And miss you loads,
But when we bring flowers,
To your grave,
We know that you are so brave.

God will keep you safe in His arms,
Where you will be safe and
Not harmed,
You can sleep in peace,
And be happy.

But we all know you'll be watching over us,
Christmas is really hard without you being here,
But we're always thinking of you,
You're always in our hearts,
And in our thoughts.

Love you Grandma.

Louise Chafer

The Butterfly

(Written by David John Rodgers on the 25.12.1997 - For his wife Maureen and given with a locket as a token of the love they share)

From an egg, an ugly little bug with hungry appetite,
Eats its way through plants and leaves all the day and night.
The cool of autumn slows it down, now the change begins.
It climbs onto an upright stem, and weaves a warm cocoon.

In autumn's rain and winter's blast, it braves the icy bounds,
A slow change within the casing mount a metamorphosis.
A mystic change of nature's charm, that moves heaven and earth.
A second chance, a fleeting life, an age, a new rebirth.

The casing splits a creature climbs into the morning sun,
The fabric starts to heave and strain, pumping life into empty veins.
Hardening in the sunbeams light, a brilliant jewel that leaps to flight.
Flutters on from flower to flower, sipping nectar hour by hour.

The pleasure as it passes by, the glorious colours of the butterfly.

D J Rodgers

I NEVER EVER HOOKED THE PIKE

The jaws' hooked clamp and fangs -
Not to be changed at this date;
A life subdued to its instrument;
The gills kneading quietly, and the pectorals.

Three we kept behind glass,
Jungled in weeds: three inches, four,
And four and half: fed fry to them -
Suddenly there were two . . . finally one -
If there was two, where is the other one?

With a sag belly and the grin it was born with.
And indeed they spare nobody.
Two, six pounds each, over two feet long,
High and dry and dead in the willow Herb - a mighty bong.

One jammed past its gills down the other's gullet:
The outside eye stared: as a vice locks -
The same iron in this eye . . .
Though its film shrank in death.

A pond I fished, fifty yards across,
Whose lilies and muscular tench . . .
Had outlasted every visible stone . . .
Of the monastery that planted him, from here and there.

Stilled legendary depth:
It was as deep as England. It held . . .
Pike too immense to stir, so immense and old -
That past night full, I dared not cast - as the water is black.

But silently cast and fished . . .
With the hair frozen on my head . . .
For what might move, for what eye might move.
The still splashes on the dark pond, pine fishing.

Owls hushing the floating woods -
Far, but frail on my ear against the dream . . .
Darkness beneath night's darkness had freed,
The rose slowly toward me, watching - pike.
In all parts, green, then green tigering the gold.

Viv Lionel Borer

DREAMS . . . WHALE AND MINE

I wish I were a whale
Swimming free with friends,
Or just born into the watery depths
By a mother who will love me for years
Who will gently carry me to
Surface air to fill my lungs
And bear me on her back when I tire . . .

As we swim the oceans together
She will teach me many things,
The only thing I will have to fear
Is ironically man . . .
Someone who is intelligent such as I
Yet destroys us from our flesh and bones.

We dive to great depths
Man, he seeks the stars!
His own planet he knows not,
Yet he aspires to land on Mars!

Or do I wish to be a kestrel?
Soaring to the heights,
Looking down on human ants
And wondering at their daily rants!

A dreamer, I believe in unicorns
And Pegasus and loving mother's arms!
Perhaps I just have to find it in my heart
To believe in things I've never had
The ultimate is love.

E Osmond

The Ill Content

I settled for an easy life,
gave up the chance of true romance,
married a sweet but simple wife,
yet never knowing true love's dance.

So we sleep in a cosy bed,
our bodies lay in a boring way,
feeling like I'm already dead,
we're unhappy every day.

I wanted something more than this,
my zombie wife and stupid kids,
All I want is a lover's kiss,
a secret, sexual, life-plot twist.

And then I have a dark affair,
with twisting tongues of passion's force,
a dirty lie that we both share,
and soon my thoughts turn to divorce.

I sauntered through my green garden,
felt the air around me harden,
plucking an apple from the tree,
I feel the chance to just be me.

Chris Williams

The Gregory Rug Co

American shadow deep twistpile - it's the way to go;
Sits wall to wall in regal style and it's looking like the way to go -
to ease my suffering,
to halve the sock washing, yeah,
to banish the chill off of icy toes - The Gregory Rug Co.

Deluxe, glue-free syrup, snug and tight, I'm satisfied,
It tidies over Duncan's blight and it's looking like I'm satisfied -
you've eased my suffering,
you've halved the leg-pulling, yeah,
you keep me free from shoulder snow; yer Gregory Rug Co.

Tom Hathaway

THE PLEASURE OF RECORDED MEMORIES

Sweet memories are stored,
Like much loved video recordings,
In the quiet recesses of our minds.
In these dark corners benignly slumber.
Their colours remaining pristine bright.
Those sunlit days of all our yesterdays.
When we deem at times to play again.
So long remain hidden from prying eyes.
Joy givers, to fill us with much delight.
Long lost snaps; youthful photographs.
Childhood play and summer holidays.
Dead relatives and pals resurrected,
Our acquaintances again renewed,
In our top ten of past events,
In the fresh open air at some county fair,
Recalling walks in a now felled woodland,
Which in later years spread to become,
An exclusively designed executive estate
On fields where we had gambolled like foals,
Planted with supermarkets and shopping malls.
Yet the reverse too, can be said to be true,
When mine workings and grimy factories,
Have over the years been demolished,
And from their debris, rubble and ashes,
Rise acres of wild grasses and pretty flowers.
Pit heaps cleverly landscaped, become wooded hills.
Though old friends and relatives are now dead,
Their young descendants in turn tread the earth.
Taking to making their own special recordings,
To play on many a quiet moment in future days.

Jonathan Pegg

I Didn't Know To Understand

The mind jumps from branch to branch
Never staying long on any bough
Takes now and then a little fall
But never down to the floor
Each bough a change of thought new ideas
Found, like buds future seeds
Among the leaves
Like the pollen impregnating, recreating,
New and pure, to open visual wide
To see a new and different point of view,
To see what sometimes eye and heart deny
The beauty of that moving sky
To think and adore, to love
To hear, to feel, to cry, to see,
The pleasures of this life, is now nee.

J L Thornton

Dancing In The Moonlight

Dancing in the moonlight
As the cool air surrounds us
Held in your loving arms
Now and to eternity.

Closer still enfold me
Feel our hearts as one
Draw me even closer
Till our souls entwine.

Let's soar up high together
Never to be apart
Feel the touch of heaven
In the clearness of the night.

Elaine Woolrich

COMRADES PRAYER

Give me a chance to make a difference
Give me the power to show I can
Give me the courage to stand tall
And lead my fellow man.

Give me the faith to carry onward
The thoughts that play within
And the knowledge to know the difference
When the game forbids the win.

When all around is helpless
And the troops fall to the ground
Give me the honesty to tell them
That help cannot be found.

For with your faith we prosper
Without your help we fail
But others lean on me
So my strength must then prevail.

J S Petch

Over You

For a while I couldn't live without her,
But now I cannot see how I was with her,
For as she said we had nothing alike,
She had her walking and I had my bike,
We each had our own separate love songs,
Something that was meaningless but still went along,
Hers by far was Gareth Gates,
Where as mine was something from Less than Jake,
Now you question if I even loved you,
But ask all the people around you,
They all knew, so why weren't you aware
That all I did was care,
You left and didn't see that you gave me a heart of stone,
But if someone is that ignorant it is better to leave them alone.

Dan Frost

SHE'S MOVED

They laughed at things that others thought
Were not a joke. They mimicked those
Who thought themselves aloof from crowd.
They plainly made each other live
With zest renewed. And yet it seemed
They'd not conceived their friendship might
Be grounds for marriage bond. They'd known
Each other all their lives and act
As sister/brother bound, not spouse.
Perhaps enigma's lack prevents
Desire from lighting fuse of love.
Or else romance requires they keep
Some secret rooms within their hearts.
But wait, he falls in love with girl
He met on trip abroad and now
They're wed. His long-time friend at last
Perceives she's been in love with him
For all those years. Too late she pines
As teenage girl with crush on man
Who teaches French at school. Too late
She sees she's lost her perfect spouse.
That's why she's had to rent a house
So far away from her lost mate.

Henry Disney

In My Mind

In my mind, there's a fire burning
In my mind, the whole world's turning
In my mind, there's love and hate
In my heart, there's pain.

In my mind, there's hopes and fears
In my eyes, there's tears
In my mind, there's envy.

In my mind, there's dreams
In my mind, there's a candle called *love*
With the brightest light you've ever seen
In my mind, there's anger.

In my mind, there's shame
In my mind, I'm sometimes happy
Sometimes, sad
Sometimes, quite insane!

Andrew Peter Richardson

FOR EMMA

Although my heart is heavy
And days of peace are few
I hope you will forgive
That I still grieve for you.

They say that I should let you go
To wander through the sky
But my little daughter
Will someone tell me why?

I waited for so many years
So I could care for you
To hold you and to cherish
With fun and laughter too.

But that has all gone now
God took you back they say
So please forgive me daughter
If I grieve another day.

Leslie Tomlinson

HOLIDAYS

Clear blue sea
golden sand
lovers stroll
hand in hand

children play
bucket and spade
picnic food
all home-made

find seashells
on the beach
overhead
seagulls screech

go for a dip
cool blue sea
big white waves
wash over me

fall asleep
on the sand
then awake
nicely tanned

ideal place
for a child
lots of room
to run wild

memories
sunny days
as into
the past I gaze.

Dianne Croskell

NORTH WEST

Nelson watchers over Newchurch
Oakenclough faraway to Ormskirk
Runcorn or Rufford quickly to Rishton
Thisleton all the way to Tottington or Thornton
Horwich way to powerful Heysham
Westhoughton, Widnes pier at Wigan
Elswick, Euxton to Eccleston
Settle to Southport sands nears Skelmerdale
Todmorden points north west triangle trail.

Lancaster of old new motors Leyland
Accrington, Adlington free parking towns
Newlonton Norbreck Nelson I see
Chorley, Claughton, Colne and Cleveleys
Abbey village, Abbeystead, Anglezarke Moor where I like to be
Samblesbury fine hall, Singleton fire station so small
Hutton Heapey, Heysham power to the all
Inglewhite, Ireby, not doing any harm
Rishton, Rossacre, Rivington barn
Elswick, Esprick, Euxton
These are some of my Lancashire yarns.

P Brewer

OLD AGE

It's no fun growing old
All you have
Are aching limbs and memory loss
Hearing aid turned up
Teeth in a glass
Specs up on the nose
Youth has passed you by
The clock ticks on
Where has time gone?
All you want
Is to stop the pain
To sleep the long, long sleep.

Alice Higham

A Trilogy Of Three

Unsigned

I search the stars eternal sky . . .
To wonder on the who and why?
Think those who've looked as I do now . . .
Who could have mastered it and how?
Who drew a curtain stitched from night . . .
Who smiled such scene of awesome sight?
Who lit the dawn with blazing star . . .
What hand was it withdrew unmarked?
Who set the planets on their path . . .
What shoulder laboured so such mass?
With not a breath of air to breathe . . .
What master he that could so weave?
I search his work to think his face . . .
Who could such labour leave no trace?

Unbound

And when I thought his face I stared . . .
Who made the stars above the earth?
I blinked and found he'd stepped aside . . .
Without his masterpiece would hide?
Or maybe it was him who blinked . . .
Wherein the cloud his face would shrink?
To stretch dissolve and blow away . . .
What portrait this that would not stay?
For I like men am finite bound . . .
Where he does go he can't be found?
By me . . . for though I ever search his name . . .
I cannot step without this frame?
That placed me in this work he did . . .
Wherein I seek without he hid?

Unhid

And yet I sense to know he's there . . .
In children's eyes I stop to stare?
Would not such souls reflect him more . . .
Unknown of stain so fresh and pure?
Like mirrors buffed to perfect be . . .
Am I so blind I cannot see?
What need to endless search the sky . . .
To wonder on the who and why?
When all the while he signed his name . . .
For eyes inside not out this frame?
For though all clay is finite bound . . .
He left His mark that it be found?
For He does glory in the child . . .
His gentle image meek and mild.

M J Banasko

ESSENCE OF NATURE ESSENCE OF LIFE

Essence of nature, the peacefulness I see
So wonderful and beautiful
as lily of the valley
Joy of comfort fulfilment of desire
Rare and sweet gently aspire.

Comforting strength of fragrance
throughout the wild
Existence of freedom, no rules to abide
Serenity of breeze gentleness acclaim
The season of bloom innocence of the spring.

Nature relies on different times of year
The so-called beauty in winter bare
At the melting of frost, the birds begin to sing
Only then . . .
Welcoming the rebirth of spring.

Assurance of hope and strength of the heart
Tranquillity of life's depression depart
Life glows, bright as the morning star
Fragrance of spring sensed from afar.

So treasure life and nature's beauty
The melancholy of time, suspended by melody
Essence of nature the chime of spring
And essence of life . . .
No longer a dream.

Cecile Maghari-Wardle

She Sailed To Freedom

The ship sailed forth into the dawn
Her sails were fully set
The waves rose high
The wind roared by
And hit her gallant deck.

Behind she'd left upon her shore
Disaster ruin pain
Brought by a foe
Whose deadly blow
Her country's life had slain.

So on she went towards the day
Her freedom she had won
But now must fight
By day and night
A foe whose friends are none.

J M Noble

IF ONLY

There's a time for work,
A time for play.
Then time to sleep but
First we pray.
And now to dream of
Pastures new, a better
Life for me and you.

Louisa Roe

Barriers And Bridges

She comes before me playing autumn song.
Windows flung wide, she sings
mournful laments in Venetian tongue
while dancing upon the water's whispered breeze at twilight.
And I (love-lorn fool of old)
hold open my palms to catch the notes
which fall as stars across the Cannaregio night.

With just a pocketful
I would build a bridge of dreams from my banks to hers
upon which she could dance me her cut-glass rainbow,
sing in my ear
songs of private pains and ice cream hearts
and how some men melt one but not the other.

I hold open my palms -
but only time slips through.
And my pocket -
my pocket is filled
with nothing but holes
lined by a ticket home.

Little girl lost, proud Persian your sole mate,
I have only these words to warm you
through winter nights and empty auditoriums

and I fear something will be lost in the translation.

Nick Milton

Natasha

It was on a warm September night that you appeared in my life,
With your dark blue eyes and porcelain fair skin,
Your rich blonde hair and secretive smile,
Taking all the emotions and love I had to give,
Unleashing a raw and passionate feeling,
Deep down in the bottom of my stomach.

Your unknowing delicate movements,
So innocent to all that see you in your glory,
Making you so important to those who meet you,
For it was on a warm and beautiful night,
That you Natasha came into my life,
For you are the most beautiful granddaughter,
That I will ever have in my world.

Sharon Tremlett

ALONE ON A RAFT

Alone on a raft
My hopes are lost at sea
What once was a great expedition
Is now only a dream for me.

The laughter and the hopes
Of what we might have seen
Are only distant thoughts
Of what could have been.

The four of us on board a ship
Full of beams of joy
Not knowing what would happen
When we reached the seas near Troy.

To Greece we were sailing
To dig up buried gold
To find some ancient tombstones
Thousands of centuries old.

Clouds of mist had gathered
Around our tiny ship
Us sailors we were terrified
Then came a massive rip.

The sails were torn from our boat
My friends lost in the ocean
The waves they towered over me
Brewing a horrible potion.

Now I'm out here stranded
Our ship is gone, abandoned.

Alone on a raft
My hopes are lost at sea
What once was a great expedition
Is now only a dream for me.

Rachel Inhester

BEYOND THE SIDE OF DAY

The stealth of night's darkness
Slowly creeps in,
Throughout the city
Night time begins.

Sleep on all you people
Sleep on through the night
Dreaming sleep's dreams
Till the dawn of daylight.

Through folds of great dark clouds
The moon shines through brightly
Whilst hiding occasionally
Behind clouds, wind blown, slightly.

The stars up so high
Give shimmering light
Across all the city
Asleep for the night.

The silence of this night
Will not long lie unbroken
As the morn light creeps in
With dawn's chorus awoken.

The birds seem to sing
Their song full of flight
Pass by all night's darkness
For the dawn of daylight.

The sun breaks through slowly
And darkness gives way
To a city awakening
With the light of the day.

The city now bustles
In the morn sun ascend
As daylight awakens
And night time now ends.

C R Slater

THE VISION OF BLUE

In the depths of December
In its dark empty days
Where the presence of winter is king
I sometimes steal moments
From the dictator's realm
And escape from the cold, damp and rain
I'll visualise a colour
Whose mood does bring joy
And the vision of blue soothes my mind
I am thus carried back
To the somnolent days
Where the blue skies of summer do reign
I fall into its embrace
Like a temporary lost child
And stare deep into the skies sapphire dome
Its presence brings me happiness
Its tranquillity brings me strength
The colour of its dawn serves my soul
Its early blue mornings
So therapeutic and quiet
When the sun and the moon shared the sky
For these moments I pine
As the dream slips away
And the dark cruel December takes stage
I return to the winter
To its sadistic empire
But my spirit is still lost to its world
My memory still lives
Neath the noble warm skies
Where the vision of blue soothes my mind.

David Bridgewater

Summer's Delight

The sun shines bright, the sky is blue,
I'm holding onto summer.
I love the sea and fresh air too,
I'm holding onto summer.
To care and share these joys with you
Is something I'll always remember.
The sun shines bright, the sky is blue,
I'm holding onto summer.

S J Dodwell

My Other Half or the Spirit of Romance

You went from here many long years ago.
But in my mind you still exist, a jewel.
Seventy-two per cent, 'twas said, have made
Contact with partners supposedly deceased.

Your visitations from on high I know
Tell me you are indeed in Heaven bright.
This is a place and state for communion
With our Maker. Where something has been made,
From complex brains to waiting galaxies,
A Maker there must be without a doubt.

This gold, painfully panned from so much dross,
We must keep secure within our truest selves.
Then, like a steering wheel, the brain can bring
The horse power of our heart's desire at last
To Heaven's portal for love's reunion.

Surely this ensures our happy ending!

Desmond Tarrant

TRYST

It's quiet at work,
There's nothing to do,
Looking at your picture,
I'm thinking of you.
Where shall we go?
Shall we go to the city?
Who's to know?
We can hold hands,
Cuddle and even kiss.
Away from where we live,
It won't seem amiss.
Bowling, cinemas even a market,
As long as we are together,
I'm sure we'll enjoy it.
Walk about town or go to the park,
It's time to go home soon,
It's not even dark.
One last cuddle, a kiss on the train,
Trying to say goodbye,
Can be such a pain.
It's time that we part,
Until we are lone again,
Tomorrow I'll nurse my aching heart.

John Batchelor

I Try To Remember What We Did

I try to remember what we did
In that first year.
We enjoyed the sun
And the waves, crashing on the shingle.
The fog where I almost lost you
And then found you, again.
Train journeys to faraway places,
Following where the rails took us.
Days spent in bedrooms,
Never caring what was outside
And then we emerged
Hungry, and dazzled,
By the sunlight,
To enjoy what remained of the day.

If I could have just one of those days
To share with you again,
I would be content.

Laura P Williams

Up

Up,
up so
high,
high in
the sky
cruising
drifting
sifting
the light
thoughts
like clouds
light and high and white
and high through places and faces and
times of telling you of my time in Peru and Egypt and those
places so far, but still near to me when I look at you I know we won't
always be here and now
I can steer
this dream
and know
that the slip
stream is
moving in
the groove
of cloud
bank and
cloud
bed to
other
places
and times
that chime with
one dream and I've
seen where we will go and
it's not where we have been.

Tim Wilson

Like Skipping Ropes And Tennis Balls

I remember us
In my history books
We were written
In all the back pages
Scribbled and torn
Out
And thrown to the floor
In crumpled balls.

As the time approached
That we were never to be
Anymore

And you broke my heart
A second time,
As I caught you giving my friend the eye
Each lunch and break times
- You would hang around
But I would ignore all your remarks
Because they were no longer made toward,

- The one you promised.
I'd be yours for evermore.

And so now we're not
And I expect you will never think or want me in the
Way you used
To hold me ever so tightly
In your arms
- Until I could safely hear
Your heart beat and pound,
Like skipping ropes and tennis balls
Hitting upon the playground floor.

Ann Worrell

My Heartfelt Thanks

We moved into our new caravan today,
And met with such a pleasing array.
Knick-knacks here and most everywhere,
Could only be done with loving care.

It was done for us whilst on holiday,
My family worked hard, I must say,
With a big help from Joyce and H,
Who worked hard with full on pace.

My grateful thanks to all of you,
Left it in your hands to see it through,
My worries taken off my hands,
As you took on such a big demand.

Thank you all once more I say,
Looking forward to our happy stay,
In a new home you did for us,
With lots of hard work, but little fuss.

Evelyn M Harding

VISIONS OF WHITBY

Standing desolate upon the cliff, eroded by time and weather,
No more the padded sound of shuffling feet, long-dead monks a relic of memory.
The ruins stare out in perpetuity at the rolling waves as they rush to meet the shore,
And the wind chants a requiem for the past through the ageing cracks and fallen stones,
Where the memories of centuries are forever locked in history's grasp.

Below the cliff, in the lee of the whistling wind, the harbour nestles close to the town,
Myriad boats, large and small bobbing gently at anchor, in undulating dream-sleep.
Silent engines, creaking decks, ensigns draped loosely round masts.
Here they wait for the men of the sea, for the return to the open ocean,
Ready to answer the call of Neptune, but for now, at safe harbour, drowsily resting.

'Twixt harbour and cliff top stand tightly terraced homes,
Stepped upwards from the lapping waves to the green and grassy cliff top.
They command a vision of the anchorage below, huddled together in secret conspiracy.
For they could tell many tales, these weathered bricks, of ships that set to sea,
And their rain-streaked panes could cry for those that never returned.

From these windows long ago, James Cook would perhaps stare and dream
Of voyages of discovery, and he saw his dreams come true.
Did he, I wonder, look down at the anchored ships, and see the world in those creaking decks?
This favoured son has gained forever his place in history,
And his endeavours, and his Endeavour are celebrated still.

And from those small paned windows looking out upon the town
Bram Stoker found his vision and Count Dracula was born.
He looked up at the ruined abbey, he stared out at the rolling waves,
And in his mind saw the wreck of the Demeter, the howling of the wolf,
Heard the screams of the vampire's victims, perhaps in the cries of the gulls, and here he found fame.

Jewel of the Yorkshire coast, treasure chest of the past,
Whitby stands and defies the rushing waves of the hungry, voracious sea, and the turbulences of man.
Still a beating pulse of the present, amidst the memories of the past,
The lights of the harbour wink at the coming of the night, a murmured silence echoes through the town,
And the decks of the gently swaying ships at anchor softly moan, and the future of a new tomorrow beckons . . .

Brian L Porter

What Am I?

You comfort me when I am cold
You'll be here when I'm grey and old
You're sometimes red, or can be blue,
But tonight, I may use both of you.
I pack you when I go away -
And use you anytime of day.
You slip into a cosy cover
And we cuddle up to one another.
By morning time you're rather cold
Not something now I want to hold.
I keep you in the kitchen drawer -
You often drip though, on the floor.
You come in several shapes and sizes
And even have your own disguises.
An elephant one lays on my bed
That's the one I said was red.
A dolphin one lays there too
That's the one I said was blue.
As I snuggle down into my sheet
I often lay you on my feet.
You must've now a good idea
'What am I?' Is surely clear.
We love you when you're nice and hot
But discard you when you're cold and not.
So, 'What am I?'
Have you guessed?
Yes - the good old water bottle is the best!

Alison Lambert

RATTIES REVENGE

Humans are a pest,
As they always butt in.
We let them have their fun,
But they think our presence is grim!

They moved on our land,
But we were here first.
So think they'll take over,
We share, what's the outburst?

Let's get them, men,
They're paranoid about us.
Listen to them scream,
And make such a fuss!

Peering through the window,
Makes them run in a flap.
Sort out their cupboards,
Nibble a hole, an escape gap!

The pickings are good here,
We have to move quick.
But much more fun,
Giving humans some stick!

A nice, warm, cosy shed,
To make our nest.
We don't mind their sculptures,
When you share, no conquest!

Ann Beard

EINSTEIN AND OTHER TWITS

Researching a log book for a missing square root,
Meanwhile savouring some hops and malt in Einstein,
Bought with fixed rate mortgage obtained online.
Napier's log and square root fell squashing my foot,
Freeing heat and energy from a relativity equation.
Fury, compared to which, aberrant nuclear fission
Seems dreary as Saturday night's repeat television.
The sequel, an interview in a nearby police station,
Where, after caution, am read my rights from mc^2.
To obtain bail will program a molecular wait
Of about twenty-two litres plus point four eight,
The volume of my cell, which alas must be shared
With Avogadro, whose quaint concept of hygiene
At NTP, poisoned the atmosphere, turning it green.

Anne Omnibus

AN OLD MAN'S DREAM

It is unfair my darling, for me to even think.
For the love I have for you, gets stronger with each
Passing week.

Although I am old.
Sometimes I want to be bold and tell you how much
I love you.
Yet, I know this cannot be
Because there are rules, for even me.

So I will just stay in the background, thinking of
What could have been.
For you, my lovely, are an old man's dream.

Norman Andrew Downie

Red

In the silent room of inner thought
I'll watch the sunrise on commercial TV
From a room without water
To a five star hotel,
I live in a place of constant extremes.
There's a man in a field working the land
While his countryman blasts into space,
Computer spaceman and farmer workhorse
Have nothing in common but the bloody red flag.
The setting sun in a hostile sky
Corrupts the world below, from its rotten core
And the tears of the mothers
Never cease, for their motherland.

Paul Willis

My Nephew

So tiny, so fragile, yet so full of life, through tears of pure joy we
Watched.
A mother, my sister, so proud we were. A father, tears stained his
Happy face,
A boy, my boy.

You grew big and strong, capturing peoples' attention with your smile,
They always smiled back.
The happiness you brought was immense, something special about you,
You didn't know it.

After your accident, it almost broke my heart, I couldn't be without
Your smile to brighten my days.
A part of me you have become and so many others - we waited.

The noise of the surgeon's drill, doctors passing us with great haste.
A mother, a father, a sister, a boy, our boy, our Alex.

Tonight I sit and watch with a thousand other eyes, so proud, my
Nephew on that stage - smiling again.
People applauding your music - and returning your happy smile.

To see you grow into a man, looking forwards to the years ahead, the
Years that might not have been.
Whatever you become, whoever you meet, don't change from being
That boy, our boy, our man.

Jil Moorehead

WAKE UP

Dad says, 'Wake up it's time for school!'
Jump into a bath like a frozen pool
I brush my teeth, I brush my hair
I get dressed and go down the stairs

Breakfast is waiting, it's toast and jam
'What's for lunch Mum?' Oh good, bread and ham
A packet of sweets and a drink of juice
And what's that other thing? A chocolate mousse

I go out the door and walk to school
And then remember the number one rule
You must have a friend everywhere you go
I have got mine and her name is Moe

Joy McFaul

LOOK UP!

Have you seen the handsome balustrade
That's set around the roof of the bank,
With its beautiful stone balusters
Standing there in support, rank on rank.

Above it there's a large chimney stack
With several ornamental flues;
An architectural perfection with
The glaze gleaming as sunrays diffuse.

A building nearby has a bell tower;
Its outline clear against the sky.
I wonder for what reason the bell rang
In this miniature belfry way up high.

And all these eye-catching attractions
Are there for each one of us to view,
But only if we raise our sights
Above eye-level; see our town anew.

For they're the work of a bygone age
When craftsmen excelled at their art,
Carving, sculpting, etching and so on,
Justly proud to have played their part.

Modern buildings don't have the same finesse;
They rise so quickly, no time to waste
On embellishments that would enhance them.
Old buildings have such quality and taste.

Marlene Allen

Baby

I know not what your name may be
Or how your face will look
A carried part of me I shall feel
Yet I will sadly be letting you go
I will never have a chance to see your sweet smiles
Or hear your first words that you will say
A little soul that lays within me I shall never forget
A cradled baby resting where my heart so near beats
I pray to God that he should forgive my soul
Little one goodbye, God bless with so much love
Lay peaceful darling, find a way to God's home.

Zoe Fitzjohn

My Scotland

When I close my eyes, what is it that I feel?
I try to make sense of it, but nothing is real.
So I let the music in and I listen, it carries me far away,
Where I feel the grass against my feet with its sway.

Oh! Please take me back to the place, where once I was free
A place that in the past was forgotten, but now I can see.
Of rolling hills, scents of heather carried by the breeze,
A time of long ago that I wish I could now freeze.

Past lives I have held and hold close to me now,
To enter once again that enchantment is now my vow.
To feel the freedom upon this darkened, lonely soul,
Where scars of this lifetime, have taken their toll.

Although I was not born of this great and treasured land,
I seek its mystical beauty to touch it with this hand.
To once again walk along the green hills like so long ago,
To breathe in its air, paddle through brooks as they flow.

Listen to the bagpipes, let the music fill your ears,
They will take you back through the forgotten years.
To feel its love, to share its wonder, to hold its mystery,
That's the gift that takes me back and lets me feel free.

Give me the bitter winters, to shiver in the icy chill,
Where this soul was once born, for it belongs here still.
Through many lifetimes I have travelled along this lonely road,
Only to end up here in Scotland where the truth shall unfold.

Nikohl Medley

AUTUMN

The giant oak stands so strong and tall,
the leaves are beginning to fall.

Leaves of orange, red, yellow and gold,
all of colours so bold.

Gliding to the ground are her gems,
revealing her upward pointing limbs.

On a bare branch rest,
an empty twig nest.

A colourful carpet covers the ground,
sending forth a delightful sound.

The rustle of leaves in the wind,
signal autumn is coming to an end.

The seasons God did arrange,
to bring about a refreshing change.

Linda Constantatos

A Deeper Love

You should really stop playing these silly games,
It seems you don't care at all,
Yet every time I pull away,
The deeper in love I fall.

You are on my mind every waking day
And all the way through the night,
But every time I pull away,
This deeper love feels so right.

As I close my eyes to sleep,
I picture your wonderful smile,
Just the thought of you makes my heart leap
And this deeper love grows all the while.

A love this deep cannot be wrong,
I so want you to be mine,
That's why I'm writing this love song,
Because I can't wait for Valentine's.

Claire Murray

Pretty Pink Rose

I woke up this morning a freezing cold dawn
I gave such a sigh, for the sun now withdrawn.
The grass is still green, the roses are pruned,
So heading for winter, I feel full of gloom.
Yet to my delight from the window I saw
The palest pink rose; its petals well formed
Alone it was standing, looking proud at its peak
No other surrounded, all pruned last week
'How did we miss it? Did the blades not cut?'
This thorny, green stem had been overlooked
A pleasure to see its fully bloomed head
A shame all the others were now lying dead.
It stood all alone looking truly serene
As if it were saying, *Look I'm a queen!*
The last of my roses such pleasure it give
No other companions, a short while to live
With winter approaching its beauty must die
Like a poetic farewell to a lovely blue sky,
Just for the winter, the roots have to sleep
To awaken next summer a glorious repeat
Once again they will give me their scented perfume
Then goodbye to winter and hale to their blooms.

Joan Prentice

POWERFUL POETRY

The spoken verse, an oral axe
Chopping through dead wood defences,
Clearing a path and sharpening senses.

The poet's pen, an ink filled knife
Carving complex keys,
Unlocking emotions, setting them free.

The poet's head, a playground for words
Bringing vision to the blind,
Thoughts, ideas, expand and colour minds.

A C Small

Tourniquet

Who can resist
the tighter the pull
the sensation
restraint
your arteries full

the time you abandoned me
left me to rot
you flowed
through
freely
left me to clot

expect me to
follow
quiet and
sincere

the heat has
died
down now
the liquid runs clear

smoke spews out clumsily
on the back of the spoon
soot distorts your image
unconsciousness
sets it soon

you intervene in my life
intravenously
that I may never forget
but watch out
for the flip side
remember

it may
pull
tighter
yet.

Lucy Reynolds

Sweet Memories

Your little life was short, yet you brought so much joy
Full of mischief and fun, yet a wonderful little boy
Then God reached down and picked you Son and replanted you again
In His beautiful garden, where you're free from suffering and pain.
Now you have blossomed Son, you send forth a heavenly love
To reach your earthly parents on the wings of a dove.

Marie Graham

Nothing Learnt

Twenty-first century man
Has learnt nothing from the past
How to destroy his neighbour
In his heart has now been cast.

The hole he has dug is deeper
There's just no way out, you see
He talks a lot about a safe new world
And of peace and security.

While he talks about such things
His mind is elsewhere
Thinking of how to destroy his neighbour
Now does that show he cares?

We vote for men to lead us
But that's a big mistake
Especially if that means death through war
Turns out to be our fate.

Someone's sitting somewhere
With an evil thought in mind
Thinking of a better weapon
To obliterate all mankind.

B Page

The Piano Is My Dream

(Dedicated to my devoted Margeret)

You place those fingers on those keys
And first the black ones give me room to please
Then all of a sudden with one swift move at ease

On goes those thoughts of thoughts of rhythm in its place
To the sparkling sound of amazing grace
As it is played voice no fears
It is magic to his listening ears

You the pianist with just accord
Leave the audience so overawed
Those fingers although they are so swift
Not one of those keys are ever missed

You can without sheet music make it plain
The terrific talent from her brain
She has hands so passion fired
Takes no time to realise it is so inspired

Then on the stool with poise and grace
As part of the piano she takes her place
With that smile of joy upon her features
Could be as though it is like when one speaks of God's creatures

And tunes of Danny Boy bring a smile upon my face
Watching her fingers glide at such a pace.

Louise A Maygwen

The Statue

Poseidon, mighty god of the sea
sits frowning on his throne,
Gleaming trident resting
bedded in the granite stone,
His mouth which once gushed water,
is now shut firmly tight
With winter's iron hard gag
sparkling in the pale sunlight.

Water which once gurgling ran
fierce and noisily free,
Now is but a frosty beard
which clothes his plinthed knee
And at his feet his companions,
four stone carved fishes white,
Leap from a crystal pool of ice,
petrified in flight.

F R Smith

SCHOOL HOLIDAYS

It's holiday time, the schools are out,
The kids just play, the kids just shout,
They laugh and scream they have such fun
Under blue skies and a beautiful sun,
Not a care in the world in these safe zones,
With their bikes and scooters and mobile phones,
They grow up strong, they grow up tall,
They play their games and of course football,
But their holidays seem to go quite fast,
Before they know it they are back in class,
The fun is over, they are back in school,
To try and learn or stay the fool.

D Cole

AGINCOURT

A thousand arrows filled the air
And still the French came on
His lordship, knights and squires and footmen too
And still the French came on
Arrows struck armour, horse, plate and chain
Straight through, the terror of the longbow
They did not really know, hundreds there before us
Outnumbered by three to one

It was cut and thrust for England, we just dare not retreat
They were pressing all around us, wounded at our feet
Hold the line with pike and steel, all were slipping in the mud
Lose your footing here me boys and you're with the Lord above
At last they began to reel, we let the captive through
Send the Duke to the rear me boys, the knight and monsignor
We come out of this rich me boys and they still come on for more
The French struck our baggage train
Henry said they must all die, we said goodbye to our fortune
For we knew the reason why
A thousand arrows filled the air, the flower of France had died
Due to the English bowmen and our
King Henry's pride.

Gatekeeper

The Child Less

When your child dies before you
Life is in reversal
A special poignancy ensues
For which there's no rehearsal.

Swept away from future years
The one to solace you in age
Bewilderment, an aching loss
A need to blame, a touch of rage

At fate, who heedless at a stroke
Wielded sword so callous-cruel
Parent should pass before the child
Obey the eternal rule.

A wisp of comfort sought and hoped
From the tears of wept tomorrows
Perhaps the chiming clock of time
May mitigate some sorrows.

Sarah Blackmore

SEARCHING

I have been searching all my life I fear,
I am not a silly person let me make that clear.
I have been to Timbuktu and across the Alps,
I have seen the native Americans and seen the scalps.
I went down the Amazon and up the Orinoco I did sail.
I've searched all over Russia but in my quest I did fail.
I've been to the Arctic, the South Pole I did climb,
But in all these places not a single one did I find.
I trekked all over the outback, saw kangaroo and geese,
I ate wriggly worms, my hosts on them did feast.
Disappointed and dismayed I ended up in Perth,
Even there I never ever found one corner of the earth.

Don Goodwin

THE MOURNING OF THE SNOWMAN

Yesterday, my pride and joy.
You patiently waited to be sculpted.
Your portly figure, well patted down, so compact and tight,
All a-glistening.
Jutted out sticks for arms, fingers widespread.
Ebony coals all buttoned up, so smart your distinctive costume.
A personality, a gift from pebbles and a carrot, a smile evolves upon.
Oh a cheeky grin!
To top it all there was Grandad's trilby, all battered but of the best
Woven tweed.

As the cockerel crows and the sun does rise,
I peek to view my chilly friend.
So sad the sight as the temperature rises,
No longer do you stand proud.
Your buttons had slid down your belly; arms now hang by your sides.
No upturned grin, but a sunken frown and the carrot is pointing south.
Grandad's trilby is cocked to one side,
I hope that you are winking!
With a sad sigh and a silent weep on this not so cold winter's day.
There's a sadness within me as I rise to the mourning of the snowman.

Mary Morley

JUST WONDERING

(For Melissa)

What will you be when you're older?
A lawyer, a butcher, a baker?
Will you work days or will you work nights?
Or will you do something bolder?

I'm gonna be a DJ,
Mixing discs all day.
Or maybe be an actress,
What do you say?

Make sure of what you do,
Don't treat it like a game
And once you are sure,
We'll love you all the same.

D Roberts

Headache

(Dedicated to my dearest friend Jayne)

What is this bloomin' din
I can't hear myself think
My head is throbbing
My pen's out of ink
I wish I could steal forty winks
Clattering pans in the kitchen sink
I'm very hot and I'm feeling pukey
I'm in enough pain to totally nuke me
The beads of sweat upon my brow
Oh there's the telephone . . . please not now
There's going to be another row
Go away you great screeching cow
I don't think I could stand the pace
To the bottle of painkillers I quickly race
In the hope it will erase - I'm reeling about all over the place
I need a dark room - and a cold flannel
My nervous tension I try to channel
But it's here and it's not budging
This evil migraine - my inner peace nudging
A chronic thumping - dizziness too
Headache you are nothing new
But I wish I could get rid of you
In the end it will send me totally round the bend
I shall be a disgruntled friend - till this corker comes
To its terminal end
And the painkillers - have started working . . .

Sally Wyatt

My House

My house is a bungalow halfway down the street,
A house that's full of happiness whose joy does not deplete.
My family is so good and kind
They all have keen and agile minds.

Its roof is brown, its walls are green
This little bungalow is supreme.
People call and knock the door
It'll stay that way for evermore.

The garden is so pleasant to see the birds fly around
The cats treading through the flowers making not a sound.
And so we sit there in the shade
As if we're in a woodland glade.

Denise Shaw

I Cut Me, I Bleed

Your lip curls up in disgust as you bind the wounds without,
But your eyes are sightless, blinkered, and give no heed to doubt.
My tattoos of pain blind you to what is me,
The cicatrices of bleached white are all that you can see.

Oh! Florence Nightingale, so valued and so loyal,
Would you be so dismissive if this blood was royal?
These battle scars I bear, mirror those I hold within,
But all that pales, to you, before my earthly sin.

What is so bad, what is it causes all this strife?
What is so bad, yet mild enough it's not worth a whole life?
Ask! Damn you! Ask! Before you cast your judgement stare,
At least show me now, that somehow, however small, you care.

You cannot cure me with your garnered skills,
But you have a mind, please help me with my ills.
Look past the obvious, use what the Lord has given,
Seek to find elsewhere, discover why my soul is riven.

This cattle grid system erodes, one more ticked off the list,
If I lay me down to die, would I even be missed?
Patchwork practice, band-aid care, no use to such as I,
I weep deep within myself, kept private from disdaining eye.

Where will it end?
How can I fill my need?
My worthless body, mind and soul,
I cut me, I bleed.

Topaz

Cruel, Cruel World

The world is cruel,
Evil and bad,
Sometimes it makes me really mad.
But it's also beautiful, peaceful and lovely.
Can you see how everything is changing,
Sure but slowly.
Every day I can see people being treated bad,
They just wanna go home to cry and be sad.
It makes me sick to see it,
Because I wouldn't make it alive.
The feelings that these people have inside,
It's just something that you can't describe.
Imagine being afraid of life,
That you just want to end it with a knife.
I promise you that it's not what you want to be,
That's why it's so important for you to see,
You can hurt someone with your eyes,
You can scar someone with your lies,
That's just something you have to realise.

Sara Ulander

The Selkie Maiden

There is a sad tale of fair Orkney Isle,
Good people fear'd for many a while,
You mathers, pathers go carefully,
Or lose your loved ones to the 'People Faerie'
As the sun went down around the shore,
A more beautiful maid I never saw,
Her skin so fine, her lips rose red,
The longest brown hair upon her hee-aad.

Silkie . . . Silkie

'Fair lassie,' said I, 'where are you from?
Such beauty's bestow'd on angels from Heav'n,
You'd make no man happier in his life
If you'll come this day with me and be my wife.'
'Three days on land, three days at sea,
Then good Sir, you may marry me,
But after that time is said and gone,
You must come with me then to my ho-ome.'

Silkie . . . Silkie

'These three days on land and three at sea
Are a drop in the ocean if you'll belong to me,
Let us waste not time here on land,
We may set forth if you'll but give me your hand.'
After these days were over and by,
The man bid farewell to his family and fair Orkney,
Went joyfully with his new wife all a'brave,
But knew not that her haim lyeth under the waa-vve.

Silkie . . . Silkie

And as they walked hand-in-hand into the sea,
He heard his mam warn about the 'People Faerie'.
'Mind the fair maidens that do dwell by the shore,
They'll steal your heart 'n' lead you into the for evermoo-rre . . .'

Caroline Schuster-Cotterell

To Be Aware

Just to stop - use the gift of sight to be aware
of nature's beauty that is there - has no need of
any spoken words, can take one's breath away,
seeing what is there.
Full grown trees covered in their own glory by their leaves
that are moved with ease by Heaven's winds.
Flowers growing wild and free add a wonder to wide open space,
and one is dawn by the many colours that they show.
Nature's world and ways are set apart from our own
busy world that has no time just to stop, then look,
take in the wonders that are always waiting there.
Our world would be a sadder place without a flower or a tree,
a blade of tall grass moved by heaven's winds,
the joy every year of a new spring, when nature's world
tells our world she is still alive.

R P Scannell

DIFFERENT CULTURES

Different cultures
tourists being preyed on like vultures
pure money madness takes the lot
feeding the machines through the slot
loads of souvenirs or just more tat
if I were at home I would not buy that
but it's not for me it's for someone else
so they can find a place for it on their shelf
no matter where you go there's fish and chips
that sit on men's tummies and ladies' hips
drinking water like it's going out of fashion
swallowing alcohol like some fanatic passion
wallowing by the pool like a roasting pig
original clothes now tight that once were too big
holiday clothes always fit a treat
but it's not the sort of thing for your local high street
lose your inhibitions and lose your senses
lose track of your pounds and other expenses
suitcases full, the money all blown
time to recover it's time to go home.

C D Spooner

In God's Lap

Quiet the day
By fireside
As the clock ticks
Time away.
Summer passed,
Autumn here
And winter soon,
It's on its way.
Another year
Of moments full,
Pleasures, pain,
Joy and tears.
Life is passing
Year by year.
Yesterday gone,
Memories here.
Thoughts of tomorrow
And what time
Will bring.
Hopes for the future
When new the spring.

Lyn Sandford

THE LOST SOUL

During the Hitler war in North Africa
in a place called Enfidaville,
I was picked to go on night patrol,
which today I remember still.

The reason I still recall this
is through an officer I will not name,
who left us out in no-man's-land
in a deed of dreadful shame.

He left the patrol to scout ahead
to find the enemy's position
and when he didn't return for many hours
we were filled with grave suspicion

That he was a prisoner in German hands,
this is what the patrol had thought,
so we decided to retrace our steps
in case we all were caught.

When we returned to our unit,
our patrol officer's sitting drinking tea.
We questioned him on why he left,
but he kept this a mystery.

Lachlan Taylor

SHADES OF SILENCE

Whenever you arise together with every twirl in every ocean . . .
rolling wave . . .
so that you may come down crashing as the rumble of the storm
of the soul.
When in the stillness of night there appear within yourself,
and flitter, the glowing ghosts of these phantasmagoric shadows.
All in all divided two by two
between the here and there of all that you are.

Michael Zammit

INDESTRUCTIBLE

Mixed emotion in a bowl
Overthrown by blindness
Deducted by force
Outcast by nature
Born without fuss . . .

Iron foot to demand
Wherever she walks
Metal queen . . .

Bland hand
Sleeping nerves never woken
Curvaceous steel
Of a living woman . . .

Shadowed mind protected
Living tissue
Of armour
Never invaded . . .

Brain of a beast
Pumped with nothingness
Belonging to a life
Of pure grossness.

Kerry Webber

Oh Youth Divine

With vigour to desire
It's wonder not to fathom
When much to utilise,
The wonder grows,
As agility grows amiss
To cope or mope
With some tenacity.

Increasing most with
Faith, that grows,
Shrinking only with neglect,
A bad contact can't connect
Its damage to restore
Oh wonder of wonders,
So wondrous with a
Pure, divine link.

Rachel Taylor

Measure Of War

The desert camp was silent - waiting,
all was still, lanterns hissed and flickered,
only movement was from the moths and gnats
attracted by the flames danced - to and fro
plans were afoot, but not for public knowledge.
The weather hot - too hot, too dry, even by night,
only movement was from the moths and gnats.
Radio silence, maintained during the sorties,
war clouds loomed large in the night desert sky.
Everything, everyone, every department, waits.
The long waits, long into a silent night,
Sound only of insects - and moths dance by lamp light,
then suddenly, action stations - scramble - roll call,
Chinooks are airborne to a secret grid ref,
all plans in action, the drop zone only known
by those who need to know - field hospital, red alert.
Thirty away, crew is airlifted out, mission done,
one half injured, one quarter walking wounded,
one third dead, one tenth unhurt, none missing.
The desert camp is on full stand by - debriefing,
the injured are treated, the crew are resting,
chaplain waits, while the dead are made comfortable.
The desert camp again falls silent - it's still too hot
and the moths and gnats still dance
to the flickering lamp lights.
All in a days work to bring peace to a troubled land.

David Charles

The Dark Coast

Over the downs of our summer sea
We roll with the wind, glad and free,
Forward looking and without fear
Of the dark coast to which we steer.

By that soldier's wind we are pressed
More hurriedly towards the west
And carry on in full career
For the dark coast to which we steer.

The following gale starts to howl,
Reserves are low, the water's foul,
When, on the horizon, sharp and clear
Looms the dark coast to which we steer.

There is no mark or guiding light,
No sure or certain port in sight,
The cliffs rise up, grim, gaunt and sheer
From the dark coast to which we steer.

In thick'ning murk we close the shore,
The seas grow hollow - hear their roar
And muffled boom, as they break near
On the dark coast to which we steer.

There's no way through, no going back,
No room to anchor, wear or tack,
No safe berth alongside a pier
Past the dark coast to which we steer.

The blind, indifferent, restless sea
Pounds to pieces the precious 'me',
Both crew and ship shall disappear
Through the dark coast to which we steer.

R J Raymond

NUMB

I walk through the ages
as the scenery changes beside me.
Modern buildings flicker
glimpses of old tradition,
shimmering in the surreal sun.
A child wanders past,
I think nothing of it
until I see his mother
dressed in creamy Victorian
splendour, with her parasol.

I feel myself flicker,
as though the centuries
are colliding,
merging and parting.

My head feels above me,
floating along in a dream,
I look at things with
years of eyes
and don't know which
ones are mine.

And I wonder if,
when the sinking sun
cools this street
and ices it over,
I will snap from this dream
and find my reality.

Jillian Shields

Is It Going To?

Is it going to snow all day?
Then I will go back to bed
Yet tomorrow it could wash it all away
Giving me a cold inside my head.

Is it going to hail all day?
Then I will go back to bed
Yet tomorrow it could rain a little
What more can be said?

Is it going to be dark all day,
Almost as dark as night?
Then I will go back to bed
Because in the dark I soon catch fright.

Keith L Powell

My Words Will Surprise!

I want to draw the curtains
I want to shut you out.
The problems that you bestow on me,
I want to scream and shout.

I want to run away and hide,
But still the shadow follows.
Your long black cloak it smothers me,
Crawls under my skin and swallows.

I cannot be your angel
I'm certainly no saint,
So please don't tell me everything,
There's some things I just hate.

I do still love you, honestly,
But sometimes I can't bear
The tales of this and tales of that,
There's some things you shouldn't share.

I cannot hold my tongue forever,
The moment will arise.
When one too many words you've told,
My words to you will surprise!

Emma Jane Tomlinson

Council Camp

We bickered in our council estate.
Concrete grazed us, while hopes
were pebble-dashed.

Full-throttle teenagers spun out of control.
No fun aged 10 -
just punch or run from those freaks.

Dads gambled little pride
on speedy hooves. No wins,
only UB40s and stale beer.
Muddle-through mums knew sanity
with cigarettes and hire purchase.

We ghetto kids escaped with demons -
only minor brain damage.

B Woods

Blossoms Of Delight

Blossoms of delight fill up the air
With perfumed beauty everywhere.
The time has come, oh Joyous spring . . .
Exuberant! Freshness, invigorating!
Blossoms of delight now fall,
Covering country, ground and all . . .

Pink petals and snowy white . . .
Spring is such a magnificent sight.

Blossoms of delight all done
In the shimmering Maytime sun.
Tiny green leaves are pushing out . . .
Hooray for Spring! I want to shout.

Carol Olson

MY CAGE

The other birds have left their nest,
Yet here am I still within this cage.
The door is left open wide,
But when I do go out, I find
It draws me back inside.
Do I like it here?
I suppose I must,
Otherwise I wouldn't stay,
I really would have to fly away.
I have a partner, such a happy chap,
He never nips, nor pecks or snaps,
Even though he seems to sleep a lot,
There are no bars around him,
So he's freer than me.
He fails to see how I'm trapped.
If I open my beak and squawk,
He just thinks I'm in a flap.
I guess the maker of this cage is me,
So I must hold the key to set me free,
But still I sit upon the perch,
Like an old hen, left in the lurch.

Pauline Uprichard

DAY

Rising sun
Sets free
The colours of the day
Germinate the fluid motion
Day gathers speed (of light)
I sleep on
Lost in dreams
What about you?

Michael Phillips

Was That You?

Was that you, Grandad, walking slowly, slowly down the road,
with weary arms, bowed over, carrying your load?
Was that you, Grandad, standing in the queue, brittle bones of tension,
patiently waiting to receive your Tuesday pension?
And as you pottered home, walking past the group
who had to have their little joke,
the wrinkled skin that just squeezed past, 'the senile old bloke'.

Was that you, Grandad, final day at work, collecting your prize
after all those years?
A watch, a whip round, a few beers and a few tears?
Was that you, Grandad, standing for your rights?
Was it really worth all those fights?
Was that you, Grandad, who no one listened to?
If they had, they would have known, that what you said was true.

Was that you, Grandad, with that baby in your arms?
Is that my mother that you hold, so loving and so light?
The proudest face I ever saw, but sad eyes, am I right?
Was that you, Grandad, coming back from that Great War,
marching through the crowds, medals worn upon your chest,
they watched and they were proud?
Were there tears salting your cheeks, as they were cheering loud?

Was that you, Grandad, 1916, a boy at the battle of the Somme,
squelching through the mud, wishing you were home?
Fighting in a war, I suppose someone knows what for.
Was that you, Grandad, crying for your friends, and praying that
the suffering would soon come to an end?
Was that you, Grandad, screaming through your pain,
cowering in that trench in the pouring rain?
And gripping tight your tortured ears, through sound of
scarlet bleeding bombs, driving you insane.

Was that you, Grandad, to whom I said farewell today,
many figures dressed in black, to send you on your way?
Though your years touched ninety and six, I still don't want this day
was that you, Grandad, who was always kind to me?
When I was sad, you made me glad, and held me close upon your knee.
And through the years as I have grown, you took my problems for
your own.

Was that you, Grandad, who gave me everything?
Goodbye, Grandad . . . watch the angels sing . . .

Stephen Young

Wild Flowers Full Of Raindrops

We had to fight for ever love,
I wasn't going to let life's cruel ways
Take your love away from me, now
That love has shown us the way to go.

Hey, hey, do you know that I love you?
Hey, hey, do you know it's the only love?
No matter if rain, or snow falls
From the skies.

So come on, we'll drive to the top of Willow Mountain.
When we get to our favourite spot, I'll turn the radio up
Just to listen to some forgotten sounds, then we will
Lay back, so I can tell you what's good about loving you.

Then we can take walks in the new moonlight,
To where some wild flowers grow, that are full
Of teardrops of love?

After a while, we can sit side by side,
Hold each moment as it goes by, then we can
Watch the city lights flicker, as we talk about
What's good about our love.

Hey, hey, do you know that I love you?
Hey, hey, do you know it's the only love I want?
Come the rain, come the snow.

Paul Wilcox

Break A Leg, Or Two

Flying saucers, extra-terrestrials, pah!
Nothing to what I've seen.
Two miracles that happened in front of me is what I mean.
Both were really gifts of God, though I never understood
Why I should be rewarded when I wasn't always good,
But I accept the role He chose for me as a leading man
And the star of the show was, of course, my wife.
The miracles were our two kids, to whom we did give life.
When the final act was over, I hastened to imbibe,
A good, stiff drink to relax feelings I just cannot describe.
Then I went down upon my knees to say my thanks in prayer
To the great producer of our successful play, up there.

Hal Takata

The Rain

A billion drops of rain
Lie resting in placid pools
Doubling the landscape
And giving the sky a twin.
Their newly found unison
Responding only to gravity
And the mortifying wind
Fresh from the Gulags.

Vaporised by the sun
The pools rise mistily
And vanish slowly
Writhing in pain from
The slow transformation
According to laws written
In the distant pavilions
Of the Big Bang.

Mike O'Brien

THE SHADOWS OF DOUBT

We never live.
We never dream.
We never cry.
We never think.

We never give.
We never scream.
We never die.
We never sink.

We are the shadows of doubt.
We have found a way out!

We never talk.
We never try.
We never win.
We never lose.

We never walk.
We never lie.
We never sin.
We never abuse.

We are the shadows of doubt.
We have found a way out!

Peter Steele

We Sailed The Straits Of Ithica

We sailed the straits of Ithica,
Lefkas to Kefalonia;
And straight ahead was Ithica,
Rising from the waves . . .
The mist surrounded Ithica
And nearby Kefalonia;
As we sailed down the Pelaga;
Honest men and knaves . . .
'Our island is rocky,
Our island is small,
But my men are hearty,
The bravest of all!'

And as we sailed round Ithica,
Our hero with his flotilla
Joined us down the Pelaga,
Creaking of our staves . . .
Singing songs so patrida;
Songs our fathers sang in war,
The wind began to blow us far,
Howling wind that raves . . .
'Our island is rocky,
Our island is small,
But my men are hearty,
The bravest of all!'

Then further down the Pelaga,
Round the Pelloponisa,
Heading north for Thracia;
Gathering like waves . . .
A thousand ships from Achia;
Sparta and fair Attica;
Along with little Ithica;
Noblemen and slaves . . .

'Our island is rocky,
Our island is small,
But my men are hearty,
The bravest of all!'

And then we sailed from Thracia;
Down the coast of As-ia;
Far from beloved Ithica;
All whom Helen saves . . .
One side - ships of Attica;
The other Lacaedemonia;
The middle - tiny Ithica;
Plunging through the waves . . .
'Our island is rocky,
Our island is small,
But my men are hearty,
The bravest of all!'

Tom Ritchie

Battle At The Proms

I saw a stage through a veil of tears
a sea of umbrellas; rain barriers
huddled, muddy people eating soggy sandwiches,
sipping white wine whilst the music played on . . .
sodden, down-trodden mad, sad music-lovers
in rain-soaked cloaks smoking smouldering cigarettes
under a charcoal-leaden gun sky
several shades of grey,
I saw the stage through a veil of tears.

The rain came heavier with each passing hour
violins, cellos, flutes . . . seemed sour
as the evening drew on, spirits fell
a music-lover's mediocrity.
Dampening dreams in a sea of disenchantment
the orchestra played 'Land of Hope and Glory'
as rain hammered like machine-gun fire
deepening dusk, husky voices
black jackets hung heavier by the hour
bedraggled children sagged with misery
I saw the stage through a veil of smears.

Rain-splattered,
shattered by inclement August weather
we sat huddled, couples cuddled under upturned umbrellas
waiting for Tchaikovsky's '1812 Overture'
fireworks fell flat as they hit the hammering rain
the last straw; a mass exodus
clutching chairs, frozen fingers fumbled
searching for parked cars, saturated,
sad, avoiding anger battling through the rain

a sea of sadness reigned as rain relentlessly fell
we staggered, bedraggle din the twilight
avoiding mud and puddles
sodden soil groaned
with bittersweet memories.

Judy Studd

ROYAL FAMILY

The royal family
Gone history of days
But remains unique
In world of ruling elements
Your uniqueness
Perfect and stranger in land of ruling
As your today's star
Remains insignificant to the world of civilisation
But stand as element of unity
The royal crown of far
The ruler of aged centuries
In history, gone and far
With unbeatable pride of time
It's a pity,
The picture, quite unrosy now
In time past
People based on tradition
And moral principle of time
Your glory, on shining crown of yours
With enormous power of perfection
Oh! Gone are the days
As nature numbs their presence
The significant presence of your glory
All remains chill in palace
But turning back the hand of time
A big joke century
Kings and queens
All remain existence of old nature
As their power remains curbed
In government of people.

Ojo Idowu Opeyemi

MISSING PERSON

I wait
And wait,
Wait, wait, wait,
For the response -
                    to my letter.

Why are you not keeping
Your promise
To always stay -
                    in touch?

You walked out of the door
Into your old life
Leaving behind memories -
                    and love.

The pain of waiting to hear from you
Is sometimes too much to bear,
Have you forgotten about me -
                    so soon?

A postcard, a phone call, a note,
Is all that I crave.
Just to know you are well and thinking -
                    and remembering.

Judy Rochester

Roy's Birthday

Today it is your birthday
And last night I could not sleep
I lay awake thinking of you
All I could do was weep.
It's been so many years now
Since you were taken away,
God knows how my heart broke
On that tragic day.
So many times in the past years
I've wondered how you'd have grown,
And if you knew who I was
You were only a few weeks old.
Sometimes I hear you crying
To awake, and you're not there,
I think I hear you laughing
But I know it's because I care.
Rest my son in peace
For I am always here
Waiting for the day
When there will be no more tears.
That day will surely be
When I am by your side,
I will be set free
From the grief I still hide.
I'll walk with you in Heaven
Sleep beside you, in peace
I need to know that you're near
For my soul to be released.
Take my hand and guide me
To you, I long to be
Until we are together,
I know I will never be free.

Till then I will wait
God will call me I know,
And through those gates
I will gladly go.

Happy birthday, my son,
Love, Mum.

T Nightingale

DIAMOND RING

It was a diamond ring
He'd insisted on it.
She loved that glittering gem
She felt like a star
And coruscated accordingly.
He had his own sparkle
But it was a reflection of hers.
It was as if the ring was a symbol
It signified their starring role
In a modern day drama of love.
Like the ring, their bond could not be broken
Their relationship was solid.
It was as hard as gold.
With both gold and diamond on their side
What could go wrong?
Theft, casual loss, wayward hoovering?

Hilary West

CHILDHOOD MEMORIES

I remember as a child that food and clothes were strictly rationed
Ladies wore silk stockings prized for being 'fully fashioned'
Our dads were in the forces fighting World War II
And Churchill made his famous speech honouring 'The Few'
In the skies giant gas balloons were ominously sailing
At night the German bombers would set our sirens wailing
Blazing fires lit up the sky - a terrifying sight
I remember blocks of houses disappearing overnight
I remember men in bright blue suits, white shirts and bright red ties
Mum told me they were wounded as tears welled in her eyes
Then the war was over, once again lamplights were lit
There were parties in the streets and everybody did their bit
Union Jacks and bunting festooned the British Isles
Laden trestle tables must have stretched for miles and miles
Precious ration coupons were sacrificed to aid
The supply of cakes and sandwiches and fizzy lemonade
Jellies and blancmanges wobbled on white paper plates
Kids poked it with their fingers and giggled with their mates
Shabby barrel organs rolled out a merry tune
And everybody prayed that our boys would be home soon
So many years have passed since then - now I'm old and grey
Yet these memories of childhood remain vivid to this day.

Jenny Hitchen

THE ARTIST

Where are the paintings of all the great men;
They live on the walls of the mausoleum.
The aristocrats, diplomats and royalty,
Hung on high walls for all to see.
Masters gave up ghosts in garrets small;
In institutions - behind closed walls.
They died penniless, often hungry, alone,
Now their pictures are priceless, privately owned.
Displayed for status show and esteem,
But a price was paid for the artist's dream
And it was not a price that money could buy;
The lines on the canvas transferred to his eye
And etched in his face feelings rare;
A suffering he could hardly bear,
But greatest of all was the artist's face,
For it bared the weight of the human race,
With eyes that looked deep into the soul
That felt all the good of the evil and foul.
For he painted a hand with brush and stroke
Sensitive feelings he chose to evoke.

Rosie Bloom

Never Go Back

I'm surprised at how little has seemingly changed
at the house with the squeaky green gate.
True, the tubs of carnations have been rearranged,
and the shed's in a bit of a state.

To see it seems odd, after so many years;
uncertain just how I react.
I remember the laurel as well as the tears
and the place where the apples were stacked.

I see that the grass is now better kept
and a porch has been built on the side
where you stood by the door and tearfully wept
and where I, too, should have cried.

There's a car on the drive, which seems somewhat new
but no cat fast asleep in the sun.
I stand and I stare but I cannot undo
the knot that was never undone.

Perhaps inside, things have stayed just the same
although I am unable to see.
The irony is, when I think of your name,
I know that this house is just me.

Peter Jones

THE ARCHITECT'S HUMBLE ABODE

He builds his handless house
with just his mind.
He imagines there's a window
and walks through dreams of doors,
each one leading to a room
greater than imagination.

His walls change with the light.
The blueprints move upon a whim.
The carpet alters with a sigh.
And still his new house rises
from the swamp of intuition,
on the building-site of mind.

This is the kitchen, he says dreamily,
a meadow for the eyes.
We agree, it smells of dinner
and lay in tall grasses to dine.
Overhead, his ceiling
is a reeling wheel of sky.

Bruce McRae

JUMPING IN PUDDLES

No jumping in puddles today
My last little one
In your black, shiny, first day
Tiny shoes
I hold your hand through the gaping
Green-railinged jaws
Of their world
Tighter than you hold mine
I feel the magic fading
The enchantment ebb away.

Brown, grubby knees scrubbed clean
Small spindly legs foal-like
Falter from me
From me?
Into their world
Pink fluorescent satchel
You wanted pink
It made me smile
My last little one
My son.

Turn around, come back to me
To me standing, shrinking
Blinking at the mist
We'll escape, run away
Fly kites that touch the sky
Find fairy rings and white campion
Come back to me
My last little one
And we'll jump in puddles
Jump in puddles - forever.

Tom May

ACKNOWLEDGE

It's noon, and cold outside
As the rain falls I wonder
Will you ever acknowledge
All the powers you possess
Through faith, hope, belief and trust
In no one else but yourself?
The long walk through life begun,
That day you entered Earth,
From your mother's womb you saw light,
A reflection of spirituality, peace and all the ups and downs
That should come, living life now from then
You should realise that you have come a long way
It's reality to have struggle
But keep strong, you are not alone
Acknowledge what you as a human can be, can do, can achieve
As they say, life is what you make it,
So you just forget the liars, the cheaters, the haters
You are in a league of your own
Leave them if you are better as one
Acknowledge this and keep focused.

M Lungu

Today

If you see me coming
better get into my way
and grab yourself a piece
of what is falling off today

I may be what you wanted
or I may be all you've got
I could be something special
only then you'd grab the lot -

But if you see me coming
then at least you are alive
those who never see me either
aren't or have closed eyes

If you are the latter
I'd suggest you look around
at what I've brought to show you
from sun up to my sundown

You may want to take off me
bird song upon a walk -
exchange virtual reality
for imaginative thought

You may see something you would
like to exchange off your shelves;
your work, your profits, wives and losses -
or your ego's selves.

And could be if you like me
you might look across your lawn
and wave to give me more yourself
as I give you each dawn.

Peter Asher

HELL IS WAITING

I can see across no-man's-land
I can see dead bodies
This is the consequence
Of rich men's power

I see the sinners
I see the innocent
Pulled off the street
Shouldn't be here

But I take mine
And wait for mine
To die in their beds
Their rich, cold beds

They are the real sinners
The ones with bloody hands
Who send people to war
Who send them to their death

Hell is waiting for them
I am waiting for them
Church can't save you now
Heaven has closed its doors.

Ali Collins

The Chester Poets

Cestrians, singers, teachers and tales,
bring me anthologies,
free verse for sale.

Pictures, paragraphs, poems and pints,
read me some lines
that'll stay in my mind.

Some time-served regional authors,
leaving images in the air;
we read poetry in the pubs,
and danced on the stairs.

We sat around like fighter pilots,
we wrote to The Times,
we listened to Celtic folksongs
and talked with our minds.

A photographer, a composer,
and writers all around,
seeing swans in the streets
of an old cathedral town.

We bought beer in the bar
and drank to the stars,
where the city met the sky,
and defined our lives.

It's high time
for writing, for drinking again;
we're a workshop, a think tank,
and so we remain.

M C Jones

THE STORM

A piercing flash, a smouldering rumble;
a crackle that splits in an outraged roar.
The crashing crack
as thunder breaks, with violent blast,
across Heaven, Earth and Hell,
then,
rain,
in deluge torrents,
and rain, and rain and rain.

In the aftermath
a well-watered lawn . . .
it was so in need,
flowers,
clean, refreshed and smiling,
fields and meadows washed, and rich in green,
the reservoirs and rivers filled
just in time to save a drought
thank God.

The rivers and waterways overflowed,
the rain,
too much, too fast
'The Storm Has Struck'
Disaster
headlines
everywhere.

The horror, the damage,
the clearing up in wet and silt;
the cleaning up of muck and slime,
the money, the waste . . .
the heartache,

The farmer's prayer?
Or disillusioned cry?
'It isn't fair.'
'It isn't fair.'
We have no hand in nature.

Diana Mudd

SEASON FIVE

Summer, autumn, winter, spring,
Nature sends sweet birds that sing.
January's weather seems unusually chilly,
February's weather blows willy-nilly.
March dithers beneath, short warming rays.
April's very angry violent storms bray.
May freezes, nature's testing
June's fledglings soon come nesting.
July's very sad, baby birds are dead,
Without August insects, they couldn't be fed.
September's breezes should have let them fly,
October's landscape was soon to die.
November, nature scrams, humans below,
December comes bearing awesome snow.
January 2050, skies are blackest night,
February's fearsome, blocks out the light.
March shudders Earth's frozen cold,
April's ferocious storm rages bold.
May trembles, nothing will grow,
June shivers, God's creations draped in snow.
Over mountaintops strange vapours swirl,
Images of nature through mist twirl
Lost across landscapes icy blue,
Gone green foliage and woodland's hue.
Cruellest sea covers lands,
Nature's awesome touch, nothing else stands.
Tell me then the seasons' mournful number,
Souls lie dead, cast asunder.
Nature has punished you for your crime,
World barren, you're lost in time.

Ann Hathaway

Slowing Down

It used to be the length of leg,
the swirl of hair,
the pivot of the lithe hip
and the white light of perfect teeth.
It used to be instant electricity,
looking up the briefest skirt
and watching that bulging cleavage
dash and wobble for an escaping bus.
But now that dog died;
grudgingly some time ago.
All that remains is a more measured man;
looking for a calmer magic
friendship; as strong as rope
unspectacular as a rainy Monday
although gentle on the human condition
and the constant throb of one's blood pressure.
We all need a quiet place
somewhere in our world
to leave our precious gems
to play in the continuous light
that the ignorant mistake for glass.

Laurence DE Calvert

THE PREY

Perching on a branch
a sparrow relaxes
looking around
seeing no danger
but unaware
a cat is stalking
ready for a meal
looking for easy prey.
The sparrow still unaware
the cat is crawling
nearer and nearer
stalking in closer.
The cat, back legs bending
ready to pounce
ready for its prey.
The sparrow
out of the corner of his eye
sees the danger
but it's too late.
The cat pounces
again the cat wins.
Easy prey
the sparrow's soul is taken away.

P Davidson

The Retired Politician

Here sits a retired politician.
Can he sense the presence of my eyes skewering through his eyelids,
Or can he no longer feel, like others do not feel for him?

He mumbles as he strides the floor, in his lonely parade.
Imaginary summits and press conferences
Once shrouded his emotions which longed to be free and young.
Will you make it? Can your lips turn upwards to smile?
His heart used to be pure, but wars that he may have caused
Have burnt holes through the muscle like cigarettes do in paper.

'I do not hold grudges, for that is unwise,' he says, and I say too,
At least we have that in common.
No, he is only human, and he tried not to lie, at the time.

He was there because he wished to make a difference,
Took one step larger than the rest of us with his determination
To attempt to bring peace, even though he saw war as the
way of obtaining it.
'How can war be the answer?' He chews his lip in self-doubt,
As once he did, long ago, sitting high and feeling so very low.

War is not an answer, but a reaction.
It is like old age, as its effects depend on how we deal with it.
'But remember,' he says, 'that I cannot remember the answer:
Is war natural?'

I'd say no, but unbiased judgement
Might be asking:
To which side do you belong?
Attack or defence?
And what are your reasons and motives?
Is war your excuse?

Dawn Marshallsay

BUTTERFLY

Aloft
On the limb
Like leaves
Swiftly
Through the meadow
Like thieves
In a group and going away
Reflecting the light
And colour of
The day.

Off with the wind they go
Caught in a drift
And loving the flow
In a stream
Straight up to the sky
As soft as a beam -
Beautiful butterfly.

High Priest

Read A Book

What sort of book
Do you like to read?
A romance or a thriller?
Or a children's adventure?

When you sit and read,
You get so involved.
Before you know it,
The time has flown.

When you learn to read,
It is such a good thing.
You can find out so much,
You can learn about anything.

To hear a child read
Is such a lovely sound.
As they read the words,
They make you so proud.

Alison Evans

Days?

What are days for?
To do your best
For fellow man
And teach disciplines
The best you can
Time and time over

What are days for?
For work and play
To see and hear
Time and time over

To touch and tell
Beautiful smells
Visions of colour
Time and time over

What are days for?
To live one's life
Full of contentment, not strife
Time and time over.

Barbara R Lockwood

All Alone

Once you were the centre of attraction
The queen bee, ruler of the castle
Love giver - advice centre - expert on children's homework
The kisser better - nobody was as good as you were
At doctoring, nursing, blowing noses, wiping away endless tears
A dab hand at cleaning, polishing
Chief cook and bottle washer, old fashioned dish washer
Launderer, ironer, fetcher and carrier
Expert shopper, gardener, decorator, builder
What ever happened to the little bit of time for leisure?
You were always on the go with never a moment for yourself
You played father and mother for far too long
It must have been really hard bringing a family of six up
All on your own - no husband to keep you company
Or to share in the responsibility of a large family
He opted for his freedom, left you like a rat
Leaving a sinking ship - you stayed, looking more worn out
With every passing day a little older
One by one your fledglings flew the nest
To better themselves and stand on their own two feet
The breadwinner did come back for a few weeks
Then went ashore for a loaf and forgot to return
Now, sad to say, you have outlived your usefulness
Living all alone in a large house
Using just the one room and clinging onto your memories
Dreaming of the past - waiting for someone to use the door knocker
Or listening for the infrequent ringing of the bell.
The telephone remains covered in a gown of dust
You wonder where your old friends have gone
Then realise most have passed on
The children, they all live abroad
So is it any wonder you feel lonely and so bored?

Eleanor Dunn

FIVE, FOUR, THREE, TWO, ONE

Off we go to some foreign shore
Taking a chance on romance.

But the rooms are not ready
And the cleaners borrow things.

We cannot sleep
Because the disco is too loud.
And in the mornings,
We have to buy water
From a shop up the hill.
Then at home, we wonder why
We ever went to Greece.

K Mood

The Proud Tree

The bleak winter,
    Sweeps in fast,
        Like lightning flashing past.
My leaves long gone, just as winter months roll on.
Snow, ice, rain up on my face, seems endless as time rolls by.
But soon the sun will warm my face, and birds will sing
the whole day long.
Bulbs peep through the grass at last.
The sun will make my leaves grow fast, and blossoms hang
within my grasp.
My blossom's full of gentle grace in the breeze do blow,
gentle in the soft wind's grace,
My tree is born again is me and when you walk beneath my tree,
you will look up and see the beauty in me.

Iris Davey

Customer Services

There seems no satisfaction,
When anything is bought,
A fridge, a washing machine or a sofa,
It all gets very fraught.

They say two weeks to deliver,
Then it turns into four,
They give no explanation,
It is extremely poor.

They ring to say the delivery
Will be on a certain day,
In the morning or the afternoon,
This they cannot say.

You wait in, in anticipation,
And when the goods turn up,
It's not the thing you ordered,
They've made a big cock-up.

You ring a number given to you,
By Tracey, Sam or Sue,
But nobody's ever heard of them,
So you speak to someone new.

They are apologetic,
But really couldn't care less,
They say that they will help you,
And sort out all the mess.

But weeks go by and nothing,
You have to ring again,
Ah yes, we have a problem,
Don't worry, we're to blame.

Meanwhile the offensive item
Is cluttering up the hall,
Just tell me when you will pick it up,
You're not paying for this call.

If you want something quickly,
It's a hopeless situation,
You must be very patient,
It'll take months of frustration.
(Usually.)

June Melbourn

Lighthouse Man

Lighthouse Man,
Pale moon's only friend.
Saving vessels from venomous rocks,
While greedy gulls scavenge fish from your ocean garden,
Squawking overhead.

Diane Bowen

POETRY ROCKS

Poetry rocks
Energise
Electrify
A force field
Of language
Poetry rocks
In sound and vision
Of performance spaces.

Poetry rocks
Transmits, communicates
Instant newsflash
Another atrocity
Pick up that pen
Instant responses
Poetry screams
Enough is enough.

Poetry rocks
Rap rhythms sampled,
It's goin' down
Poetry shouts
Hey man! What gives?
Are you makin' the scene?
Are you living your dream?
Hey man, you know what I mean?

Poetry rocks
S' cool
S' alright
Poetry be
Your friend tonight
Look deeper
Into its light
Poetry rocks.

Ian Bosker

Will We Remember?

Will we remember the garden of midsummer?
Children at play amidst a sea of flowers
Around the peaks, gentle monsoon mist
Enveloped our hearts with Heaven

Will we remember tall trees so old?
Those lines each curve shaped in grace
Such green and wild perfect each beat
As morning hours rolled to afternoon

Will we remember the hush of the storm?
Butterfly's dance across the wheat field
Will we remember the way nature called?
Will we remember our love being born?

Simon Kilshaw

VENNY, BARBADOS 1974

(Dedicated to Vannessa Forest, friend from my days working at the Midland Hotel, 1972 to 1994)

Salome danced for Herod
On his birthday; joyously,
He said she was a gift,
And pledged her anything:
'Anything?' she smiled.
'Anything!' she looked at
Her mother and said . . .
'I want the head of John
The Baptist!' The courtiers
Laughed, as John forgave
His executioner: 'I forgive
You: I shall live again,
In Heaven, forever!'

Edmund Saint George Mooney

AWAKENINGS

Lacking, something is lacking.
I'm tasting dust,
Rusty emotions lay prickly on a cardboard wash.
Too many people in one room,
Gathered to speak of me.
Me, my mind
Me, my future.
Me, not giving a damn,
But I'm here in this room
Closing and locking the door
Climbing into a bed.
Closing my eyes
Where dust has settled in corners.
And I wake, wonder . . .
Rain beats shapes into my heart,
Though I know I'm only walking through
To a new dream . . .
To find a new horizon
To find a fresh start
To find a harmonic hue.

Josephine Kohl

The Inner Life

It does not seem
that life's precise;
Within a scheme
it does not seem.

Until you've seen
the inner life;
It does not seem
that life's precise.

Frank Murri

Love On Earth

Perhaps soon the corners of the Earth shall meet
At a central point, and stop, and know
Once and for all that He is here
And there's no place else for us all to go.
Except with Him, as He encircles the globe,
Gathering the universe in His hands;
With Him, as He lights each star en route
And yearns for us all to understand
That He alone, deep within us all
Must rest, abide . . . and be the only goal
For us all to seek and to want, and know.
None other than He . . .
Then love on Earth, shall flow.

Blanche Helena Hall

A PERSONAL GENESIS, A QUESTION OF GENETICS

In dreams, I tread the boundaries of subconscious reality,
And, in a haze of unbidden confusion, ask the question,
'Who am I?'

The blood of two continents flows through my veins,
Colouring the ocean of my soul,
Aztec and Tarascan, conquering Conquistador,
Images which flood my mind, in the half-world of my sleep.
I hang upon the edge of memory, trying to see beyond the veil,
But it hangs there, blurring the images of the dreams.

Memories of ancient rites, of colours and of words,
Words of ancient meanings, languages long-gone,
The sights and scents of a world apart flood my sleeping thoughts,
They absorb my soul, until I wake, and they are lost again,
And all the reminiscences of genetic memory cry out in unison,
'Who am I?'

For I am the sum of many parts, but the past is indistinct,
Who can separate the bloodlines of a dream?
Conqueror and conquered, two turbulent pasts entwined,
Within the seeds laid long ago are the answer to my question,
So am I the progeny of history, what was the genesis of my dream?
Am I East or West, am I the New World or the Old, for my history
is both?

In dreams, I hang upon the edge of memory, and almost touch the truth,
But I am many nations, many people, and the dreams are indistinct ,
the reality obscure,
So will I ever find the answer to my question, 'Who am I?'

Juan Pablo Jalisco

SLEEPING GIANTS IN SUNDAY BEST HATS

In the desert of Sonora, in the heat of the afternoon,
I witnessed nature's hand at work, though it was over much too soon.
In this drought-parched barren landscape, I came across a giant,
Accompanied by many smaller companions, though all entirely
self-reliant.

For three long years she had stood there, living on nothing
but her reserve,
Now at last the signs were good, maybe a chance for her future
to preserve.
Her skin was dry and hard, and scorched by the unrelenting heat
of the sun,
And the giant waited, patiently, maybe knowing what was
about to come.

A subtle change in the air above, and the sky began to change its hue,
Clouds of white and purplish-black replaced the powder-blue.
Orange-yellow streaks of lightning cut a swathe through
the gathered cloud,
And peals of thunder echoed through the sky, growing ever nearer,
ever loud.

The cavalry of charging clouds gathered pace in the darkening sky,
Approaching the standing giant, who waited, patiently, and oh so dry!
A final peal of thunderous rage and the sky was rent as though
by the sound,
And a cascade of life-giving rain began to fall on the stony
desert ground.

The lightning cut through yet more clouds, ripping holes
in the angry sky,
You could almost hear the giant drinking, anxious not to let
this chance pass her by.
Before long, with grim predictability, as quick as it came
the storm was gone,
And the giant stood there once again in the glare of the afternoon sun.

But now life was different, the rain had rekindled the land,
And the giant, and all those around her, as if aided by some unseen hand,
Sprouted forth upon her head a blossom of the wild,
As though giving birth after all this time to a long-expected child.

A perfectly formed white flower, the yellow centre, proudly sat
Upon the top of the forty foot cactus, like a delicate Sunday best hat.
And all the giant's companions joined in this great parade,
And the desert was filled with nature's colours, oh what a sight it made!

In too few days the flower was gone, and with it, all the others,
So the giant returned to sleeping in the sun, along with her sisters and brothers.
She would stand in quiet serenity until the time when the thunder would roar,
When the lightning would rend the sky and the rain would bring life to the desert once more.

Maria-Conchita Moreno-Jalisco

Song For Natalya

(Stalingrad 1942)

Natalya, my Babushka, shall I ever see you dance again,
In white swansdown and flowing lace, captivating the hearts of men?

The world is going mad little one, amidst the snow and ice of our
bleak Russian winter,
Our city is nothing but shattered ruins, where the bones of the dead
crack and splinter.
Bombs and gunfire all around, and the living just live to die,
And the smoking ruins of our beautiful land send their funeral pyre
up to the sky.
Freezing fingers stuck to metal, toes diseased and black,
Fighting for each building, one street forward, another one back.
Bullets rip like angry wasps, through bodies too numb to feel,
Bodies of old men, women and children, joined in patriotic zeal.

So Natalya, my Babushka, shall I ever see you dance again,
In white swansdown and flowing lace, captivating the hearts of men?

The motherland is freezing, gripped by ice and snow,
But still the bombs and gunfire rage, and the buildings of our city
burn and glow.
And who will live to tell the tale of our heroic stand?
Who will sing the songs for us, we who fought to defend this land?
Upon this stage of white on white, the blood stains a darker red,
I wish for only the chance once more to sleep warm in
a comfortable bed.
I dream of the time when the guns are silent, when the snow
begins to thaw,
But all that reality has in store is bombs and bullets galore.

I wonder, Natalya, my Babushka, if I shall ever see you dance again,
In white swansdown and flowing lace, captivating the hearts of men.

The faces of the starving haunt my every waking hour,
The sound of another sniper's bullet echoes from the ruined tower.
My feet are just two blackened stumps now, boots perished days ago,
And every step I take in this awful ballet of horrors is oh so painful,
oh so slow.

I shall never dance with you again, hold you aloft above my head,
I think perhaps it won't be long before I am counted amongst the dead.
I'm so cold my little angel, I must lie down here in the snow and sleep,
I feel so very little, but I think that last bullet penetrated very deep.

So I'm afraid, Natalya, my Babushka, that I, your Nikolai, will never
see you dance again,
In white swansdown and flowing lace, captivating the hearts of men . . .

Vladimir Nikolai Vetchinsky

THE DAY THE WORLD STOOD STILL

It was when the Princess of Wales was killed in Paris in a tunnel.
The driver of the car was drunk and doing 121 miles an hour!

This lovely woman was a saint in every way.
She started by launching a fight to get landmines banned
in all countries.

Every month they kill 1200 people and maim 800.
Many are children. These children deserve a life.

She loved everyone: lepers, people with AIDS, people with no
hope in life,
people living in cardboard boxes on London streets.

It has all been so sad. Two weeks later Mother Teresa died.
Diana said she was inspired by her.

This was a tragic shock for the whole world!
She brought light to the darkest parts, and hope where there was none.

I have never known or seen such grief -
millions of people, of all races showing so much emotion.

We shall never forget the tragic loss.

James William Milner